UNWANTED
DEAD OR ALIVE?

UNWANTED
DEAD OR ALIVE?

Greg Seaver

Unwanted, Dead or Alive

Trilogy Christian Publishers A Wholly Owned Subsidiary of Trinity Broadcasting Network

2442 Michelle Drive Tustin, CA 92780

Copyright © 2024 by Greg Seaver

Scripture quotations marked NASB are taken from the New American Standard Bible® (NASB), Copyright © 1995 by The Lockman Foundation. Used by permission. www.Lockman.org. Scripture quotations marked KJV are taken from the King James Version of the Bible. Public domain.

No part of this book may be reproduced, stored in a retrieval system, or transmitted by any means without written permission from the author. All rights reserved. Printed in the USA.

Rights Department, 2442 Michelle Drive, Tustin, CA 92780.

Trilogy Christian Publishing/TBN and colophon are trademarks of Trinity Broadcasting Network.

Cover design by: Jared Seaver

For information about special discounts for bulk purchases, please contact Trilogy Christian Publishing.

Trilogy Disclaimer: The views and content expressed in this book are those of the author and may not necessarily reflect the views and doctrine of Trilogy Christian Publishing or the Trinity Broadcasting Network.

10 9 8 7 6 5 4 3 2 1

Library of Congress Cataloging-in-Publication Data is available.

ISBN: 979-8-89041-529-5

E-ISBN: 979-8-89041-530-1

Preface

The cover of the book represents the song "Unwanted," which I wrote several years ago. I will tell you, in one of the chapters of this book, how the song came into being. The chorus of the song talks about where an outcast man (myself) finds commonality with Jesus.

Unwanted, that's who I am.

Unwanted, an outcast man.

I heard You (Jesus) were rejected too.

Everyone had abandoned You.

Like me, Your Father turned away.

And Your friends, when You died that day.

You were unwanted.

The image on the "Unwanted" poster cover is of Jesus, who was a Jewish man. He was pursued by the Jewish chief priests in Jerusalem. They plotted to have Him killed. They hired one of His disciples, Judas Iscariot, to identify Him with a kiss in the garden of Gethsemane in the dead of night. They paid Judas thirty pieces of silver to betray his rabbi. Jesus had entrusted Judas with the ministry's money box. Judas was a thief who pilfered some of the money from the box (John 12:6, NASB).

Have you ever felt unwanted? Or maybe you were betrayed by a kiss? I felt that I was unwanted very early in my life. That feeling looked as if it was never going to leave me. There were also some kisses along the way. You will have to read my story to find out if I got free from my feelings of rejection. You will find out why I came to believe that I was unwanted.

You may want to know what is meant by *Unwanted, Dead or Alive*? First of all, it is referring to Jesus. Some say that He didn't rise from the dead after His execution on the cross, that His body was stolen and buried elsewhere. Over five hundred witnesses say that they saw Him after He arose from the grave on the third day. Secondly, in Ephesians 2:1 (NASB), Paul said, "And you were dead in your trespasses and sins." So, if we all died in Adam, can we live again (Romans 5:12, NASB)? John wrote to the church at Sardis in Revelation 3:1 (NASB), "I know your deeds, that you have a name that you are alive, but you are dead."

Introduction

I want you to know that I was born with something unwanted inside of me. Over the course of my life, this evil insider would compel me to commit spiritual crimes against my will. Those crimes have the possibility of convicting me to an eternal death without the possibility of parole. I became an unwanted man who was guilty until proven innocent.

You are about to turn the page. I need you to pay attention to the crimes that are being committed by me against some of the people in my life. These people were close to me. Others were total strangers.

As I describe to you some of the pivotal scenes in my life, I used flashbacks to help you understand them more fully. These scenes are pertinent to help you see that I deserve everything that I have coming to me. I italicized them so you would know when you have entered a flashback. I returned back to using regular font once the flashback had ended.

When I was a little boy, I would cry to try to avoid getting a spanking. This usually happened when I had been found guilty by one of my parents. They would be standing over me, ready to punish me for what I had done wrong. Sometimes, they had compassion on me. Thus, they wouldn't strike me very hard because I was already crying.

There's something else I must share with you before you embark on this journey with me. There are unseen forces at work in my life. Some of these forces are good. Others are evil. They are invisible, but you can catch glimpses of them. Their voices are manifested through various people in my life. Some speak blessings, and some speak curses.

Hopefully, you will see that I was living in a prison most of my life. There were times I escaped, but some malevolent prison guards would find out where I was hiding. They would come and drag me back to my cell.

On judgment day, I will be standing before the Righteous Judge. I am guilty, and I know it. I will not be able to cry enough tears to get out of this one. But, if I cried out for mercy, would He have compassion on me? Does He hear me when I cry? Is there any hope of avoiding the eternal death sentence that awaits me? You will have to read to the end to find out.

1

I was sitting in my bedroom reading a book on the second coming of Jesus. I was halfway through the book when I understood that I was a sinner. I knew why Jesus had died on the cross for me.

"Jesus, Jesus, Jesus," I whispered as tears began forming in my eyes.

My heart began to burn with a warmth that I didn't have words to describe.

Almost immediately, I went looking for my father. I found him lying on our couch in our living room. I reached down and hugged him.

"Dad, I love you!" I said as I squeezed him tightly.

It may have been the first time I had ever uttered those words to him. I don't believe I had ever told myself that I did, let alone him.

Until that night, I had hated him for most of my life.

I was nineteen years old.

When I was much younger, probably around eight years old, I walked into our garage. My dad was in there working on his car. He was hidden under the hood of the car, so I couldn't see his face.

"Hi, Dad! What are you doing?" I said, trying to get his attention.

"Get me a wrench out of my toolbox," he said without greeting me.

I began searching until I located his toolbox. I froze as I looked down inside of it. There were many tools in there. I didn't have a clue as to which one he wanted.

"Which one of these is a crescent wrench?"

He stormed over to where I was standing. He reached down and snatched up the one that he needed in a fury.

"You are a sissy like everyone says! Go on, and get out of here!" he said in a disgusted tone.

My eyes filled with tears as I walked out of that garage and away from my father.

My mother was someone I admired growing up. She was beautiful and appeared to be strong. It seemed as if she had the power to gain control over my dad. Sometimes, she would yell and scream to get her way. She would even cuss at him as a last resort if she deemed it necessary to get him to do what she wanted.

One day, Dad and I (just the two of us) were getting into our car to go somewhere.

"Why do you tolerate the ugly way Mom talks to you sometimes?"

"I usually just try to ignore her when she gets that way."

"I don't think I could ever let someone talk to me the way she does to you."

Don't ever let anyone control you like that, I said to myself while I was feeling sorry for my dad. He changed the subject of our conversation. I left the subject of my mom alone for the time being.

I had a thirst to know God, even more than my quest to know my dad. I read every book I could get my hands on about Him. I sponged in book after book, trying to get to know Him. I could feel His presence at various times. I could feel a warm sensation in my chest when it seemed like He was talking to me. I would feel another kind of sensation on my hands and other parts of my body when I prayed or talked to Him.

I fell in love with the One who had died for me. The One who had formed me in my mother's womb. I learned that my mom had been a month pregnant with me when she married my father. This meant that I had been conceived in sin. I wouldn't find out this truth until much later in my life. My father's parents weren't happy that my dad married a divorced woman with three kids.

2

I began dating a girl who was a Christian. She usually attended church with her family every Sunday. I started going to church with her. Her pastor was fiery with a fire and brimstone style to his sermons. He had a kindness underneath the fierce way he preached. I would sit forward in the pew as he preached, taking in every word.

One day, I was at my girlfriend's house. She and her mother were discussing what she was going to wear to an upcoming dance at her school. She was seventeen and still in high school. Anger started rising up inside of me. I felt like she and her mom were trying to control me, and I didn't like it. I walked out of the house to get into my car to leave. She ran and opened her front door to ask me what was wrong. I told her I was breaking up with her. I left her standing in her doorway with tears streaming down her face as she watched me drive away. I tried later to reconcile with her, but her parents forbade her to do so. They believed that I was worldly and not a good influence on her.

Let me take you back to the beginning of our relationship. We had been on three dates when I finally got up the courage to kiss her. She kissed me back but laughed afterward.

"Why are you laughing?" I asked because I was uncomfortable.

"I thought that maybe you were gay because you hadn't tried to kiss me until now. I am relieved that you finally did."

"No, I am not gay," I said as I started laughing too.

Another time, we were making out in my car. I moved my hands from her waist to try to feel her breasts. She immediately grabbed my hands and moved them back down to her waist. I tried one more time, and the same thing happened. I quit trying.

I am not sure that kissing a girl and then trying to feel her up makes me worldly. I am not sure why her parents thought that I was. I decided to respect her parent's wishes, so I stopped trying to get her to go out with me again.

I don't think I was that worldly, but I wasn't innocent either. I had lost my virginity to a girl when I was eighteen years old. She was a friend of mine. I was staying at her house with her and her family. The reason I was temporarily living with them for a few weeks was because she and I were planning to attend a volleyball camp together. She had helped me get a job where she worked so I could save up enough money to pay for the camp. My family lived several hours away from where she was living at that time.

One night, she and I were standing face to face in her backyard. I had playfully gotten on top of her in her bed just a few nights earlier. I had to sleep in her bedroom because the other ones in her home were occupied by the rest of her family. That night, we both laughed as I began to make some thrusting movements with my hips pressing against hers. It started out as innocent fun. My smile quickly left along with hers. We both noticed my thrusts had begun to be transformed due to some sexual desire apparently starting to rise inside me because it had manifested on the outside too.

"You better get down and sleep on the floor. I will make you a pallet," she said, trying to convince me that I should stop before things went any further.

I did what she wanted. I covered myself up with a blanket on the floor. I smiled again as I thought about what had almost happened. I drifted off to sleep.

Now, we were in the dark once again, but this time, she was the one making advances.

"Why haven't you made any more moves on me since the other night?"

"I didn't think you were interested in me because you had asked me

to stop."

"No, I am interested. If you do some things that turn me on, then we can have sex."

She led me around to her front porch. It was hidden from the outside world because the shrubbery that was planted around it had grown up tall enough to hide anyone laying on it.

She questioned me to see if I was enjoying what she was doing. I told her I thought I had already enjoyed it too much because of the sensation that went through my entire body. I was a virgin. I had never even masturbated. She looked at me with a disgusted you-must-be-kidding-me look on her face once she realized I had already had an orgasm. We walked back into her house without either of us saying a word. None was needed because her face told me that her first sexual encounter with me wasn't at all what she had hoped it would be.

One night, after I had broken up with my girlfriend, I was out drinking with a man whom I had met at work. He was a co-worker of mine. He was several years older than me. He was married but was currently separated from his wife. When we got back to his house, he invited me to stay the night.

"You are way too drunk to drive home. I'll call your mom to let her know you are okay but that you are going to crash at my place. You can sleep in my bed with me if you want because my couch isn't very comfortable."

"That's fine with me," I said back to him.

I was slurring my words. I knew if I had called my mom, she'd know that I was drunk, and she'd be upset. I sensed that his desire for me to sleep in his bed with him was something more than just about my discomfort. However, I was too drunk to protest or even care at the time. Besides, I had some curiosities about some of the feelings and attractions I had been feeling towards men.

Once we were in bed, things gradually led to where we kissed and explored each other's bodies. That's all I remember because I passed out. I woke up the next morning feeling sick. It wasn't just because of all the alcohol I had consumed the night before. I got dressed and tried to run out of his house as fast as possible. On my way out, he tried to assure me that what had happened the night before wasn't a big deal.

"Greg, are you okay? Don't feel guilty about what we did. I am not in love with my wife. I am sure we are getting a divorce."

"I am not upset. I just need to get home. My mom is going to be worried about me if I don't hurry up," I said in hopes that he would step aside so I could leave.

On my drive back home, I was bombarded with some guilt and confusion about what had just happened the night before. A part of me wanted it to happen, but now I was really upset and confused. I vowed to stay away from him so that I wouldn't give in to my curiosity again.

A week or so later, I was resting on my bed in my room. I could hear my mom talking to someone in the other room. My body tensed up when I realized it was my male coworker.

"His bedroom is just down this hallway," my mom said to him.

I was in bed because I had been sick. I had missed some days at work. He was at my house to check on me because he thought there might be more than just me being physically sick. He was right, but I had no intentions of discussing my feelings of confusion with him.

He shut my bedroom door behind him. He studied my face as he began questioning me.

"Are you okay? Are you avoiding me because of what happened with us the other night?"

"You can't be this crazy right now? Keep your voice down so my mom doesn't hear you!" I said in a hushed but stern tone.

I got out of my bed and was up in his face to make sure he had heard me. I must have had quite a look on my face; it should have told him that I wanted to punch him in the face for having the audacity to show up at my home! He took a step back away from me and looked into my eyes.

"It's okay if we fall in love with each other. There's nothing wrong with it."

"No, it isn't okay. You need to leave now," I said as I pointed toward my door, motioning for him to leave.

After he left, my mom came to my room.

"Wasn't that nice of him to come and check on you to see if you were alright? He seems like such a nice man. I am glad you have a friend who cares about you."

If she really knew what was going on, she would have lost her mind.

Let me interject something here. I felt in my conscience that what I had done was wrong in my sexual experiences with both a male and a female. I felt the same kind of guilt each time. However, I didn't let my guilt stop me from having sex again with a woman or a man though. I wound up having sex again with my volleyball friend while she was on a break with her boyfriend. I stayed away from my male coworker until after he got divorced. I went out drinking with him again. This time, it ended up with us going all the way once we got back to his apartment.

3

Just because I had broken up with my girlfriend, I hadn't broken up with God. I continued to pursue Him. I kept attending my ex-girlfriend's church. I decided that I should get baptized because of my faith in Jesus. My family came to witness the event that Sunday morning. After coming up out of the water, I had a warm sensation from my head all the way to my toes. I was filled with a joy that words cannot describe.

I began writing poems about God. I stood up in our church and read one of them one Sunday morning.

"It looked like a halo was around your head as you read your poem to us," said one of our deacons.

I was on cloud nine. Some people told me they thought I was going to be a preacher. They would comment on the anointing that they said they saw on me. Others would say, "You sure have a way with words."

One day, my pastor asked me if I would preach a message for our congregation.

"I want you to speak for us at an upcoming service designated for our youth."

"I don't know how to preach, but I am certainly willing to give it a try," I said in agreeing to his request.

"I have a sermon outline book. I will let you borrow it. It should help you come up with an idea for the service."

The sermon book didn't help me much.

You got saved while reading the second coming of Jesus. Maybe if you talk about His coming, someone else might get saved? I thought to myself.

The sermon topic was settled in my mind. I was going to read a passage from 1 Corinthians 15. Paul wrote a letter to the church at Corinth telling his readers that those who believe will all be changed in a moment, in the twinkling of an eye. This will happen when Jesus returns for His believers.

I was standing behind the podium at my church. My parents were there to support me. They were seated to my left on the second row. My grandmother (who was a Christian) was sitting in the same row along with one of my sisters and one of my brothers. My brother had brought his girlfriend with him. The choir began to sing the song "Learning To Lean On Jesus," and that's what I did that morning.

I had been praying to God for six months in hopes that He would save my family. I wanted them to experience Him in the way that I had been experiencing Him. I never dreamed that I would be the reason why they'd be back to church again. We had attended some church services when I was younger.

One morning, during one of those services, my mom told one of the preachers that I had something to say during a time in the service when some people gave their testimonies.

"I love Jesus!" I said with the biggest smile on my face.

"That's wonderful to hear, son," the preacher said as he smiled back at me.

Now, I had been telling almost everyone about my faith, including most of the people who came up to my window at the bank where I worked as a teller. Some smiled. Some disagreed that I hadn't been saved because I hadn't been baptized at the same time. Some disagreed because I hadn't been baptized in Jesus's name yet.

"You need to read the book of Acts," one man said with a grumpy tone.

"I don't have time to teach you, but you have a lot to learn in order to be saved," another lady said to me with disdain on her face while shaking her head at me in a condescending way.

I thought everyone would be happy that I thought I had gotten saved. I was definitely wrong in making that assumption.

I stood up behind the podium at my church, and I read the passage that I had selected to start my sermon. I began describing what I had been experiencing over the past few months with God. I told everyone that I had attended a similar youth night at my grandmother's church. I said I had seen something that was different on those teenagers' faces that I had never seen before until that night. It was something that wasn't on my face then, but it was now.

"I understand why they looked the way they did that night. Jesus is living on the inside of me, just like He is in some of the teenagers at my grandmother's church."

I ended my talk with an invitation to anyone who would like to get saved. I closed my eyes in prayer as the church choir began singing "Just As I Am."

I opened my eyes just in time to see my mother and my father get up out of their seats and step into the center aisle. My mother was crying. Her right hand was over her face as she was trying to hold back her emotions that were now erupting out of her eyes. My dad put his arm around her as they made their way to the altar to pray. He was crying too. They were about to meet with the God who had saved their son.

My legs buckled underneath me. It was my turn to release an eruption of emotions. I began crying out to God.

"Thank You for answering my prayers! Thank You for saving the ones I love most in this world. I love You so much!"

My sister, my brother, and his girlfriend also got saved that morning.

"I had a burning sensation from the top of my head to my toes. I almost knocked the people down who were standing in my way. I couldn't get to the altar fast enough!" my sister said, telling me what had happened to her in the service.

4

One night, I met a girl who worked in a fast-food restaurant that I often frequented.

"How's your girlfriend doing? I can't help but notice she's not with you tonight," she asked with a concerned look.

"We broke up. It didn't work out between us."

I walked towards the front door to leave. When I got to the door, I turned back around.

"I am available," I said with a smile that suggested that I was ready to try again with the right person.

"I am available too!" she said with a smile that let me know she might be the one.

She was an attractive girl with a funny sense of humor. She had dark hair and dark brown eyes. I was happy to learn that she was a believer in Jesus.

My grandmother's pastor called to ask me if I would come and preach a sermon for their church. Word had gotten out about what had happened at my church when my family got saved. I didn't tell you, but just about everybody in the church was in tears that morning. There was shouting and exuberant joy on display for all to see. Many told me to keep preaching as I stood at the door with my pastor, who was thanking them for coming to the service.

The Sunday that I was to preach at my grandmother's church arrived. I stood up in front of the congregation. I read out of the Bible and prayed for God to speak through me. When I opened up my mouth to start speaking, my mind went blank.

"It seems God doesn't want me to preach this message. He must have a different one in mind," I said laughingly while I seriously searched inside myself to find out what He wanted me to say. The congregation politely laughed with me as they waited to see what I was going to say or read next. I read another Scripture. I started to speak, but I went blank a second time. I was confused, and I started to get embarrassed. It took everything I had not to sit down.

God, did You call me to preach, or did my church call me? We need to have this conversation, but now is not the best time, I said to Him on the inside.

"I guess it's not that one either," I said with a laugh while trying not to cry.

To my surprise, the congregation waited patiently again. When I opened my mouth the third time, the sermon began to roll out. Thoughts flowed from my head to my mouth as I proclaimed to them about my relationship with God. I kept speaking until I instinctively knew that it was time to stop. After I was finished, I went and sat down next to my girlfriend. She smiled at me, but I didn't smile back. I had determined in my heart that my second sermon would be the last one that I ever preached.

I was sitting in the car with my girlfriend after the service was over. She could see something was really wrong with me.

"Greg, what's wrong?"

"I am never going to preach again! I can't believe that I went blank twice before I finally started hearing something to say. I am never going to embarrass myself like that again!" I said to her as we were facing each other. A look of disbelief came over her face.

"Greg, you can't quit. God called you to preach, and you are good at it! When you started to speak the third time, I began blinking my eyes because everything began glowing around you with brilliant light. Your suit transformed into a bright, shiny one!" she said with big eyes full of wonder.

"Wow, you really saw that happen?" I asked.

She nodded as she squeezed my hand, which she was holding.

I became encouraged by this vision she was sharing with me.

"Okay, God, if You still want me to preach, then I will," I whispered inwardly with amazement on my face.

Thirty-three was the number of times that I preached that first year of ministry. Here's what would happen. I would get an idea for a message downloaded to me by the Holy Spirit. Not long after, someone would call and invite me to come and preach at their church. Usually, I asked my girlfriend to sing for these congregations before I preached. She could sing like a professional vocalist. Sometimes, I would sing too. Many people thought my singing was awful, but they didn't say it to my face. I could tell on their faces that it wasn't very good, but they were speechless.

Things were going great in our relationship. We were two young people in love. We wrote love letters to each other. We had given each other nicknames too. Most of our dates consisted of us going to church services, gospel concerts, or church revivals being held in our area.

One day, my girlfriend sat me down.

"I have something I need to tell you," she said while she tried to compose herself.

I could tell she was afraid to tell me what I was about to hear. I smiled in a way to let her know that she could tell me anything.

"I think I am pregnant," she said with dread in her voice because she was wondering how I would react.

"Are you sure that you are?" I said without falling out of the chair where I was sitting.

"Yes, I am pretty sure. Thanks a lot, Greg! This isn't how I was hoping you would react."

My thoughts went running as I tried to redeem myself with

her. How was I going to tell everyone that this so-called preacher had gotten his girlfriend knocked up? After I finished burying my ministry calling, I asked myself this question.

Is this someone that I would want to spend the rest of my life with?

I nodded to myself that she was definitely that person.

"Let's get married. Will you marry me?" I asked.

"Are you sure that you want to get married to me?" she asked with some skepticism. "I don't want you to marry me if the only reason is because I am pregnant!"

"I love you, and I want to spend the rest of my life with you."

She smiled with joy, and so did I. We hugged and set out to tell our families what we were planning to do.

We were sitting in our pastor's office. We had asked him if we could meet with him about something very important.

"We want to get married as soon as possible. Will you marry us?" I asked.

I watched his relaxed face shift to one of uneasiness due to the urgency in my voice. He rocked back in his chair and looked at the both of us.

"It would be my honor to marry the two of you. You both look so in love. Because Greg's a preacher, I don't feel like I need to counsel you two. You have my blessing," he said to us with a warm tone in his pastoral voice.

I breathed a sigh of relief that he had agreed to move forward with our plans.

We held hands at the altar as we sang "There Is Love" to each other at our wedding. We were standing up in front of the altar at the church where I had preached my first sermon. My bride-to-be never looked more beautiful than she did that afternoon. Our family and friends witnessed two young lovers tying the knot with joy beaming on their faces.

My wife had told me that she found out she wasn't pregnant right before we were married. I was happy that we were marrying each other for the right reason. She was happy that I still wanted to marry her. I was glad that my reputation had been spared. I loved to preach, and I didn't want my ministry to be over because I was having sex outside of marriage.

It rained the day we got married. My mother smiled at her future daughter-in-law, who was making final preparations with her dress before walking down the aisle.

"Do you know what they say about when it rains on your wedding day?" my mom asked.

"No, what do they say?" my bride asked.

"For every raindrop that falls, it is a tear that you are going to shed. I am sure it's just a silly old wives' tale. I hope the ceremony goes well."

My mom left her to go into the sanctuary to find her seat. She was about to watch her baby boy get married.

5

Not long after we were married, my wife announced to me that we were going to be parents. We were both twenty years old at the time. I had mixed emotions about becoming a father. I was concerned about how we were going to be able to afford a child. I didn't make that much money in my current profession (banking), and she made a modest wage at her job too. I was also concerned that maybe she was pregnant when we got married, but somehow, she was unaware of it. We were probably going to be the talk of the town, but not in a good way. Some people asked us questions about what the date was when we got married. They began counting the days until my wife delivered our first child (especially our church members).

My wife was standing in our bathroom with a look on her face that I wouldn't soon forget.

"What's wrong?" I asked as I was about to slide by her to relieve myself. I had just gotten out of bed. It was very early in the morning.

"My water just broke," she said with a calm voice.

"I have to take a quick shower before we can leave to go to the hospital," I responded.

She rolled her eyes as she went to change out of her wet clothes that had just been soaked.

Back then, my hair had to be perfect. I couldn't go anywhere without it being in place. Not even to take my wife to the hospital to give birth to our first child. I am sure you are probably rolling your eyes too. I don't blame you.

Our son was born eleven months after we were married, if you were wondering. It was one of the happiest days of my life. I had this incredible joy that you couldn't put into words even if you tried. I drove home to pick up some things my wife had forgotten to bring to the hospital. She should have had enough time to get what she needed while I was in the shower, right? I am just kidding. I am sure she was filled with anxiety about going through the pain of birthing someone into this world. Warm tears were flowing down my cheeks as I thanked God for giving me a healthy son.

6

Three years later, God gave us a second son. The circumstances surrounding this pregnancy were quite different than the first time we were expecting. Let me begin by saying that my wife had slept with a high school sweetheart while I was staying at my parent's home for a few days. I had been shocked to learn the news that she had been spotted at a restaurant with another man. I confronted her about what I had heard. She looked surprised that I knew she'd be on a date, but what she told me next took the breath out of my lungs.

"I slept with him," she confessed to me. Then, she asked me not to hate her for doing it.

How could you do that? I thought you loved me? I said to myself, but not out loud.

I walked out of the room in disbelief.

Before you start feeling sorry for me, let me tell you what I did while I was away at my parents' home. My wife and I had been having some marital problems. I needed to get away, to process how I was feeling about her, about us. On one occasion, she had smacked me across the face during an argument. Anger rose up inside my heart, but I didn't smack her back. I didn't even think of doing that because I was in shock. I slammed the door as I left our apartment that night.

I was at a shopping mall in the town where my parents lived. I noticed a man staring at me. He smiled as he walked by me. He turned around to see if I was watching him walk away. Before he turned back around, he flashed another smile at me. He walked through the mall doors to the outside parking lot. I took off quickly to follow after him. By the time I almost caught up to him, he stopped at his car. I walked up to him, and we started making the usual small talk when you meet someone for the first time. Then, he asked me a question that confirmed why I thought he had been smiling at me.

"Do you want to come back to my place?"

"Yeah," I said because that's all that I could manage to say. I was so nervous.

I was upset with my wife, but how could I hold her in contempt since I was guilty of sleeping with another man too? I didn't confess my sin to her. I didn't dare. I forgave her, and she seemed very glad that I had. I doubted very seriously that she would have forgiven me if she knew what I had done.

We consummated our reconciliation when I felt the Holy Spirit in a different kind of way afterward. I had felt His presence in the same way one other time after we had made love. It was around the time she got pregnant with our first son. I believed that God was letting me know that it just happened again.

"We just got pregnant!" I exclaimed.

"Huh? What do you mean?" she asked while looking at me like I was crazy.

"I felt the Holy Spirit in an unusual way after we made love. I have only felt Him like this one other time before. It would have been around the first time that you got pregnant."

A short time later, she told me that she was pregnant. I began struggling to believe what I had originally prophesied about her condition because she had slept with an old boyfriend. My doubts caused me to pull away emotionally from her. The stress of everything we were going through probably was the cause for her getting sick. She had developed toxemia and preeclampsia. Her body swelled so much that you could push an indention into her legs easily by using your finger.

At eight months into her pregnancy, she had reached a dangerous point. Her doctor induced labor, and her baby's heart rate dropped. They rushed her away to prep her for an emergency C-section while I rushed to the hospital chapel to pray. I cried out for God to save my wife and baby. One of the hospital staff found me, and he took me to the operating room. I was there to behold my second son's birth and hear his first cry (I was in the delivery room when my first son was born). God had answered another prayer of mine.

My wife and son came through the delivery safely, but they both had complications. She had a kidney crimp. Therefore, she had to stay in the hospital for two weeks. Our son had to be in a special care nursery because he had been removed from his mother's womb prematurely. It was difficult to see him inside an incubation chamber with wires attached all over his body to monitor his health status. I reached through one of the holes in the chamber. He grabbed my finger and my heart at the same time. Tears began streaming down my face. One of the nurses came over.

"Would you like to hold him?"

"Would I ever! Yes, I want to hold my son."

She took him out very gingerly. Then, she carefully placed my son into my arms. My heart melted even more as I prayed over him to my Heavenly Father. I thanked Him for the miracle I was holding. His skin coloring was a lot like mine. In fact, he even had some of my mom's features. His features would develop into looking more like ours over time. He would wind up having her beautiful big brown eyes too. It was miraculous that our marriage had survived the storms of both of our infidelities.

My mother took our son home with her a week later, while my wife remained in the hospital another week.

I was so happy when I was finally able to bring my wife and second son home.

Not long after they were home, I received a call from a church to come and preach a trial sermon for them. I felt very comfortable at this little country church when I preached there for the first time. It felt like I belonged there. This church unanimously voted me to be their pastor. I gladly accepted their offer. Then, I quickly became concerned. So, I prayed to God.

"God, how am I going to come up with a sermon every week for these kind folks that You are calling me to pastor?"

Now, I was twenty-four years old. I had a wife and two kids. I was working fulltime at a bank. My plate was full, but so was my joy.

7

"Greg, why have you been coming home with smoke on your clothes and booze on your breath? Where have you been going?" my wife asked.

I didn't want to tell her the truth because I believed that would be the end of our marriage. I sat there in silence as she continued to grill me with questions.

"Is it another woman?" she asked.

"No, it's worse than that!" I said as I began to cry. "I don't want to hurt you. I don't think you could handle the truth!"

She looked as if she was thinking to herself, *What could be possibly worse than my husband cheating on me with a woman?*

"Is it a man?" she asked, fearing that might be the reason for my late nights away from her.

I desperately wanted to tell her that I thought I was gay. I had been going to a gay bar in another town where I had grown up. It was about an hour and a half away from where we were living at the time.

The first time I went to the bar, I was too scared to go in. I watched a few guys go in while I was sitting in my car. My fear of being found out was great. Not only was I a married man, but I was a pastor of a church. How could I even think about risking my marriage and my ministry? But there I was, sitting in the parking lot.

Suddenly, a guy came out of the bar. He seemed to be looking around for some unseen guest. He pulled out a pack of cigarettes and put one in his mouth. I opened the car door and moved out of the driver's seat. I shut my door loudly in hopes that he might hear it. Then, I leaned up against the hood of my car.

"Aren't you going inside?" he shouted.

"Nah, I don't think so," I replied.

He walked over and introduced himself. He was a handsome man with dark hair, dark eyes, and a really nice tan. Before I knew it, we were headed back to his apartment.

After putting my clothes back on, I confessed to him that I was married.

"I'd weigh two hundred pounds if I was a heterosexual," he said *laughingly.*

I was surprised at what he told me next. He began trying to persuade me from being gay.

"It's a hard life. You have to constantly stay slim and look your best all the time. I have had lots of boyfriends. I just broke up with someone. It gets harder each time that happens. You should go back home to your wife and stay with her if you can," he said with conviction.

I deflected his intervention efforts by changing the subject.

"I am too scared to go into the bar by myself."

"I will take you if you are afraid to go there alone."

"I would appreciate it if you would."

I guess he gave up quickly on trying to change my mind about being gay, huh?

I was about to break the heart of my wife by sharing with her the truth about my late-night escapades.

Was our marriage going to be over? If I tell her the truth, will she divorce me? I can't keep living like this, though. This lie is killing me, but the truth may kill our marriage.

These thoughts, along with others, were running quickly through my mind. I mustered up the courage, and then I blurted it out.

"I think I am gay!"

I began crying harder as I unraveled emotionally while I was bracing myself for the rejection that I believed was coming.

She sat there looking at me with a puzzled look. Then, she uttered the words that I never thought I'd hear in a million years.

"I can handle it."

What did I just hear her say?

I was dumbfounded but also relieved that she didn't say that she wanted a divorce. I caught her looking at me several times the next day after I had revealed my secret to her. She was staring at me, but it was as if she was looking right through me. It seemed as if she was trying to figure out why she hadn't seen it before.

I had worked hard on trying to hide the fact that I was attracted to guys. I remember a movie that my wife and I had watched together. It was about a married man who began sleeping around with men. He and his wife had a very similar relationship as we had.

"This is disgusting. Are you okay with this movie?" she asked.

"It's okay. Let's keep watching it."

She looked at me strangely. Then she turned her attention back towards the television.

That wasn't very smart on your part! Are you an idiot? I said to myself.

I didn't want anyone to know because I thought everyone would reject me. For some reason, God hadn't rejected me, and now my wife hadn't rejected me either.

Handle it was an understatement, as you are about to find out. She seemed to possess some kind of extraordinary resolve inside of her that ordinary humans do not possess.

However, neither of us knew about what kind of rollercoaster ride we were about to get on. She embraced the truth about what I had told her regarding my sexuality. I was about to move forward with my pursuit to find out the truth about who I really was. My father said he never saw me do anything with mediocrity. This gay matter would be no different than any of the other pursuits in my life.

8

Five years ago, God asked me to write my unwanted story. Our conversation about writing it went something like this.

"God, how am I going to write a book? I don't know anything about writing one. I have written songs and poetry, but a book? And how am I going to remember the things that happened in my life decades ago?"

"Don't worry, I remember everything. As you write, I will help you remember the things you have forgotten. I want you to get up tomorrow morning at four a.m. to start writing."

"God, do You know that I am not a morning person? Is this really You? Well, it has to be You because I would never tell myself to get up that early, especially just to write a book that I don't even know how to write."

I was up early the next morning because I had to use the bathroom. I glanced at the clock. It was four a.m. I was sitting on our white porcelain throne in our bathroom when my conversation with myself was interrupted by God.

"I am so tired. I can't wait to get back in my bed."

"If you don't write this book that I am asking you to write, then I will find someone else to do it!"

"Okay, God, but You have to help me."

"I will. Go sit at your laptop and make out an outline. Use the twelve songs on your 'Unwanted' CD as a guide."

I obediently followed the instructions that He gave to me.

It took me several weeks to finish the first draft. The first version of my story was written in third person. It fell short of what I believed that God wanted the book to accomplish. I gave up trying to write it.

A few years later, I began to write the finished version that you are reading. During that time, God began to show me that He had put a writing ability inside me that I would eventually come to believe was in there.

Just as all rollercoasters eventually come to slow down and stop, mine does too. They stop so anyone who wants to get off their ride can safely depart. If anyone wants to stay on, they can as well.

I am not sure why you picked up this book. You may have been attracted to the cover. Someone may have given it to you to read. Have you ever felt unwanted? Please keep reading if you have. I pray you hang on until the very end.

9

I was sitting at a man's apartment, looking at him holding a piece of paper in his hands. We had been seeing each other for a few weeks. He looked intently at me to make sure that I was paying attention to what he was about to tell me.

"There are over thirty names of different guys on this paper. They are all the men I've been with up to this point in my life. The last guy, before I met you, gave me a sexual disease. It ended our relationship because I could no longer trust him anymore after he did that to me."

"I am sorry that you had to go through something that heart-breaking."

"It's okay. I just want you to know that this life you are pursuing isn't easy. If you can make it work with your wife, I highly recommend that you do so."

It was obvious to me that he wasn't in an emotional place to start another relationship because he had just been devastated in his last one. I appreciated that he was being honest with me. I wasn't happy about what he was saying between the lines. His efforts to open up my eyes were unsuccessful. I had feelings for him, even if he didn't feel the same about me. I was in uncharted territory. My heart was having a hard time understanding what was happening.

My drive back home was anything but easy. I was chastising myself for being so dumb to fall for another man.

Maybe I should take his advice? The first guy that I met at a gay bar (parking lot) tried persuading me to avoid this gay life too.

My wife could see I wasn't myself when I walked through the door. I dismissed her concerns as I headed off to our bedroom. I wasn't about to tell her that I had fallen for another man but that he didn't want any part of a relationship with me. With my back turned away from her, a tear rolled down my cheek. I was emotionally exhausted. I finally drifted off to sleep. Before I did, I told myself a few things.

"Please do not make this same mistake again! It hurts too much. Is it possible to just have sex with someone and not develop feelings for them? Apparently, it must be because the guy who had just broken my heart seems to be able to do it."

The fear of being hurt slowed me down, but eventually, I went back out to the bars because I thought there might be someone out there for me to love.

10

You might be wondering about the church I was pastoring. I fell in love with those people. God was faithful in giving me a message every Sunday to preach. They called me brother Greg.

I was amazed that I could still feel God's presence with me, even though I was sinning by having sex with men. Not to mention, I was committing adultery. Even more surprising to me was that He would still speak through me. God loved those people I was pastoring much more than I did. It wasn't their fault that I had fallen into this sexual pit after a year of preaching God's word to them. He was faithful to them even though their pastor was in sin.

"God, why did You call me to preach, knowing I was attracted to men? Please take these feelings and desires away from me!"

I prayed like this, tearfully crying out to Him on many occasions. I wanted to serve Him because I loved Him. I wanted to pursue men because I had a burning desire that wouldn't let up. I was in danger of losing a congregation that I loved. I loved my family and didn't want to lose them either. I didn't want to die prematurely, but that was a viable possibility. AIDS was a roaring epidemic at that time. Many gay men were dying of this dreaded disease. I don't know what you would have done if you were me. But I had no intentions of slowing down, even though I could be risking my own life.

Right out of the blue, something happened to me that I didn't see coming. I found someone to love at another gay bar. This time, the feelings were mutual. This guy I met would set up an avalanche of beliefs for me that were just about to fall.

I believed that I was gay.

I believed that being with a man was the only way I would ever be happy.

I believed that I needed to tell the rest of my family members the truth about my life. I believed I needed to confess to them who I really was.

I believed that I was about to break my wife's and sons' hearts.

I believed I was about to break God's heart too.

I would probably be walking away from His call on my life.

I didn't want to be a hypocrite standing behind a pulpit telling people about God and His Word. I was living a lie while trying to tell people His truth. To be honest with you, with myself, that's who I had become, and I hated it.

God rained down fire and brimstone on Sodom (Genesis 19). Many people say that God hates homosexuals. We are the worst of sinners in many people's eyes, especially some ministers. They seemed to forget that in the flood, God destroyed all of mankind except for Noah and his family. Maybe they haven't forgotten, but I guess it's easier to target sins that you aren't committing. Do you think my theory has any validity? I can tell you that not too long after my conversion at age nineteen, I had my own judgments about other people. I became very religious and condescending. It's as if I had a spirit of religion (better than thou) that was causing me to condemn many of those around me. I am not sure how this came about, to be honest. Maybe it was some sermons I had listened to. Or even a demonic spirit?

I still felt God's loving presence even though I was gay. I believed I had found someone whom I could be happy with for the rest of my life. You'd think I would have been ecstatic. A big part of me was hopeful, but I was feeling like I had this unbearable weight on top of me. I still needed to tell my parents. I had no idea how they would react to the news of their son being gay. I wasn't feeling rejected by God (although I feared that He would change His mind). Maybe my parents will not reject me either?

I was about to find out because I was on my way to meet them.

I was a nervous wreck, to say the least. I tried to believe everything would be okay once I told them the truth.

My parents were two people who had already been through so much in their lives. Because I had seen them go through hardships, and I also knew what they had been through early in their lives, I had tried to be the best kid I could be growing up.

My dad had a rare bone disease when he was a young boy and almost had his leg cut off because of it. He had dropped out of school at a very early age because of this disease. He became a workaholic in the field of carpentry. He was someone who had worked very hard to support his family.

My mom lost her mother while she was trying to give birth (the baby died also) when she was just a little girl. She grew up never knowing her biological mother or father. Her aunt and uncle adopted her. Her uncle tried to molest her. At the age of fifteen, she married a man to get away from another one. After having three kids, she told me that she began to hate her husband. She got divorced. Sometime later, she met my dad.

When my mom was about to give birth to me, she thought she was going to die just like her mother. She started bouncing her hips on the delivery table, thinking if she kept moving, then maybe she wouldn't die. She didn't die that day, but the news she was about to receive would just about kill her.

My father, my mother, and I were all sitting in their car. It was dark outside. I was seated in the back. I was struggling to get any words to come out of my mouth.

"Greg, what is it you need to tell us? Just say it," my mother asked.

By now, she was growing impatient due to my hesitancy to let them know what I needed to tell them.

I don't really want to do this, but I need to be honest with them. I took a deep breath and slowly let it out.

"I think I am gay."

Immediately, both of my parents started wailing and sobbing.

"Are you sure?" my dad asked while trying to recompose himself.

"Yes, I am sure."

I was surprised by all the emotions that erupted so quickly. I cried almost as much as they did.

"Your wife called and told us that you were going to tell us that you were gay. She was afraid we wouldn't be able to handle hearing the truth come out of your mouth without being somewhat prepared to hear it," my mom said.

I didn't think that it was my wife's place to tell them before I did. Seeing how they reacted, already knowing what I was going to share with them, I believe that she did the right thing.

"Let's go inside and sit down," my mom suggested.

We were in the parking lot of a restaurant. I didn't know why anyone would want to eat at a time like this.

My mom looked me in the eyes. There was a pain in hers that I never want to see again for the rest of my life.

"I'd give my life to change you," she said as tears began to manifest her anguish once again.

She continued by saying that on one occasion, when she had driven by the gay bar in town, she had a premonition that one of her sons was in there. She thought it might have been my oldest brother because he wasn't married.

I would have been her last choice because I was married with two boys. Besides this fact, I was a preacher.

"Son, wouldn't it be a good idea to see a counselor to talk about what you are going through?" my dad questioned.

"We will pay for it," my mom said in the hope that this offer would help sway my decision.

I was baffled by what was happening.

Why aren't they just accepting the truth? I know who I believe that I am. Look at what I have already been through in determining what I now believe to be true, I said to myself.

I pondered their proposal for a moment.

I do have some more questions about homosexuality, so maybe I could get those questions answered by seeing a counselor? I said to myself.

"I will go and talk with a counselor."

We got up to leave. I was relieved they hadn't rejected me. My best scenario would have been that they also embraced me being gay. That hope of mine was lost. They were two fighters who had been through many conflicts.

They were praying for a miracle that their son would change. "God, thank You for helping me face one of my greatest fears," I whispered.

11

I was sitting in my counselor's office. She was a beautiful, compassionate woman with a very warm smile.

"What brings you here to my office?"

"I am attracted to men. My parents thought it would be a good idea for me to come and see you. I want to try and understand why I am the way I am."

"I am glad you are here. I will do everything that I can to help you."

She began asking me questions about myself and my relationships. She was easy to talk to at first. I felt very comfortable telling her some truths about myself. It was difficult to try and not twist my words to make myself look better. I resisted the temptation to do this in the beginning. I had never told the truth about myself to anyone, but here I was telling it to this beautiful stranger. I guess, deep down, I wanted to tell someone. At the end of our first session, she gave me a cassette tape to take home and listen to regarding homosexuality.

I eagerly put the tape into my cassette player as soon as I got in my car. I couldn't wait to hear what was on there.

The speaker began by saying that he used to be a homosexual. He told about how he had struggled with his sexuality until he found some answers in the Bible. He referenced a statement the apostle Paul had written in his letter to the Romans in the Bible.

"Reckon yourselves dead to sin, but alive unto God in Christ Jesus."

How do you reckon yourself dead like Paul had instructed his readers to do? I wondered to myself.

The speaker described himself as someone who lived in a house made of mirrors. In other words, everywhere he looked, he saw himself.

"I live in one of those houses too," I told myself.

He was married to a woman like I was. I understood some things he said, but a lot of it didn't make sense to me.

My counselor and I talked about the tape at our next session.

"What did you think about the tape?"

"I liked it. It gave me some understanding, but I am not sure how to apply it."

"You will need to be patient. You are just getting started on your way to recovery."

Over the next few weeks, she gave me some more of the speaker's tapes. I was always quick to listen to them.

She gave me some books to read too. One was about the road less traveled. The other one was about caring enough to confront someone. She thought both books would help me in my marriage. She focused a lot on my marriage. It seemed like she thought if she could fix my marriage, then maybe I wouldn't be gay anymore.

I would always feel better after our sessions together. But that was about to change in a hurry.

One day, my counselor met me at the entrance of her office. Normally, she would be sitting at her desk in her office when I arrived for our sessions.

"Greg, I have invited another counselor to sit in with us today. Are you okay with him being in our session?" she asked.

"I guess it's okay," I said while I shrugged my shoulders.

The counselor greeted me with a firm handshake. He seemed nice enough, but I immediately didn't think I was going to be as comfortable talking to him in the way I was with her. She led us down the hallway into his office. We all sat down together.

"Greg, the reason I wanted all three of us to talk is because this man has had some success in helping other men deal with their homosexual feelings."

Her statement helped me to have less anxiety since I now knew that he had talked with other men like myself.

He began leading our session. He looked at me squarely in the eyes.

"Greg, you are trapped in a state of double binds. You are in love with a man but married to a woman. You are pastoring a church while living in sin."

I looked at my counselor. My face told her that I wondered how he knew all this information.

"Like I said, he has had a lot of experience with your issue, Greg. I consulted with him about you because I had never counseled anyone who believed they were gay until I met with you. I wanted to provide you with the best help that I could find for you. I hope you don't mind that I shared your story with him?"

It's a little late to be asking me for my permission! I thought.

I looked back at him to see what he was going to say next.

He told me that day would be their last day to see me unless I decided to put all my relationships on hold, including the church I was pastoring. It was as if he punched me in the gut. I thought about putting on my poker face, but he had already shown me his cards. It was too late for me to try and bluff my way out of this hand that I had been dealt. I looked at her. She was clearly on his side. So, I laid my cards face down on the table in front of me.

"It looks like I do not have a choice. I will do what the two of you are asking of me."

"You are in an impossible situation because of these double binds. We believe this is the only way you can have the ability to objectively choose which direction you want to go in your life," he said, with her nodding in agreement.

"I want to give myself the opportunity to receive any help the two of you can give me," I said while trying to believe the words that were coming out of my mouth.

I don't understand what double binds are completely, but I know what being double-teamed means!

I didn't say that out loud, but I wanted to.

They both smiled at me as if trying to reassure me that I was doing the right thing. I waved goodbye after scheduling my next appointment with them.

I left, shaking my head in disbelief about what had just happened.

"How am I going to tell my boyfriend that we need to take a break? Will my church understand that I need to take a 'break' from being their pastor? I believe my wife will understand because she wants me to get beyond my homosexuality."

I felt like I was myself when I was with my boyfriend. I loved my church. I didn't want to hurt any of them. I want my wife to be happy, but I don't think I am the man that can make her happy.

"God, please help me put all these relationships on hold except Yours and mine! I won't be able to do this without You."

My boyfriend, my church, and my wife all agreed to put our relationships on hold when I asked them. My boyfriend struggled as he tried to smile to say that he understood. My church leaders looked concerned when I asked them for a leave of absence. I assured them that I was okay. I just needed some time away for personal reasons. I told them that a preacher buddy of mine had agreed to fill in while I was away. My wife looked surprised by the counselors' request but agreed to do so even though she wasn't completely on board with the idea.

Shortly thereafter, my break to freely pursue God and my healing were interrupted by my mom.

"Greg, aren't you any better now that you've been in counseling?

My parents were paying for my therapy. If you remember, they were the ones who encouraged me to go.

Anger rose up inside of me.

"I am better but not healed yet!" I snapped back.

"How long is it going to take?"

"I don't know how long it's going to take!" I said as I walked out of the room away from her.

My relationship with my mom would have been described by her as a good one. She confided in me about her life, her relationship with my dad, her fears, or whatever might be plaguing her at any given moment. When I tried to talk to her about being gay and what I was going through, she would quickly shut me down. If I said anything about liking something, she would question my motives. For instance, I told her about loving to play volleyball.

"I hope you aren't playing it to try to impress the boys."

Are you kidding me? I thought while rolling my eyes.

Looking back, I can see that she was only trying to help in the way she thought was best. It was obvious to me at the time that she was never going to be for me what I had been for her.

I decided that I was going to stop my counseling. I was upset by the way my mom had questioned me about it.

"Didn't she know that I wished it was that easy? Go to a few counseling sessions, and all your problems are solved in no time at all. Really? If it were only that easy!"

At the time, I assumed it was about the money. I believed that she wasn't getting what she was paying the counselors to do fast enough. I should have realized she was a mother who desperately wanted her son to change. Remember she said she'd give her life to change me? I must have forgotten that she had said that to me. I will never forget the look in her eyes when she said those words to me.

After my break was over, I decided the best thing would be for me to break off my relationship with the man I loved. It was very hard for me to do this, but I believed that it was the right thing to do. I went back to my church to resume being their pastor. My wife and I started working on our marriage again.

My anger towards my mother hadn't subsided, so I called my counselor and told her that I needed to see her right away.

The following week, I was sitting in front of her in her office.

"How are you doing?" she asked as she smiled in a way that only she knew how.

"I am not doing okay. I am upset with my mom. I am going to stop my counseling because she doesn't think I am getting the help I need fast enough. My parents are the ones who are paying for me to see you."

"Greg, you aren't ready to stop counseling. You're not healed yet. Don't stop if money is the issue because we have a sliding scale. Can't we try and work out the financial details?" she pleaded.

Her concerned eyes were filling up with tears.

"My wife and I can't afford it, even on a sliding scale."

"I wish there was a way that you could continue working with us."

"I am afraid there isn't at this time. Thank you for all you have done to help me."

Now, there were tears in my eyes as I stood up to shake her hand and tell her goodbye. I turned away and slowly walked out of her office.

12

My wife began going to Christian bookstores in search of any books on homosexuality. I began searching for books as well. We found several on the subject. I read them as fast as I could.

I listened to many testimonies from men who had supposedly been set free from their unwanted desires. Over time, I began to get some hope back.

I learned about how my homosexuality may have developed, but these revelations weren't bringing about the change that I ambivalently desired.

Eventually, I returned to giving in to my homosexual desires once again.

One day, I met a man who was a minister. During our conversation, to my surprise, we wound up talking about homosexuality. This man told me that he wanted to start a support group.

"I have a lady friend who is dealing with lesbianism. I'd like to start a group that could help her and anyone else who is struggling with this issue that wants to attend."

"As a fellow minister, I would like to learn more about helping people. I think it's very admirable that you want to help. To be honest, I have had some similar struggles as your friend."

"I don't struggle with this issue, but I had an encounter with a man a lot earlier in my life. I believe that I have repented of it, but I may have some unresolved feelings. I still think about it from time to time."

He told me that he would talk to his friend about getting together as a group.

"I will let you know what she says."

"I look forward to hearing back from you. I am really interested in learning more about this subject. It would also be good to have an opportunity to discuss what I am going through."

Later, he called me up to let me know that she was interested in starting a group too.

"You must agree to keep this confidential. She is very nervous about anyone finding out about her secret struggles."

I understand her fears. I must have some of the same ones that she does, I said to myself before responding back to him.

"We all need to feel safe about sharing our stuff. I don't want anything I share in our meetings said to someone else outside of our group either," I said in my agreement to keep everything confidential.

With everyone on the same page, we set a time to meet to get started.

At our first meeting, everyone seemed nervous and awkward. The minister told us, her and me (there were only three of us in the meeting), that he thought we should approach our problem like an addiction based on how we seemed to feel at different times when our desires surfaced. This approach would follow a twelve-step program like Alcoholics Anonymous. Instead of admitting we were alcoholics, we would admit to being same-sexaholics. She and I agreed with him that he could be on to something.

We admitted out loud together that we were powerless over our same-sex struggles (the first step) at our next meeting. I wasn't the only one in the room searching for answers as to why I was addicted. After counseling sessions and reading every book I could get my hands on, I was still left standing in the dark. I could see this same kind of helpless feeling in the eyes of the lady sitting next to me. My heart ached for her as she searched for the courage to open up to another human about the darkest places of her soul. The anguish on her face and the tears in her eyes told me more than she ever really wanted anyone to know. She had demons that were tormenting her. She was looking for something or someone to deliver her.

After several weeks, we completed all the twelve steps. Step four required us to take a moral inventory of how our addiction had affected ourselves and the people in our lives.

It was very hard for me to look at all the pain that I had caused everyone, including myself. My quest to quench this burning desire deep down in my soul had caused so much heartache in so many people that I loved. This step was designed in the hopes that by looking at the devastation, one would have the motivation to never do something similar again.

The twelve steps didn't bring about the changes in us that we hoped they would. The minister proposed that we read a book on pursuing sexual wholeness and use the workbook that accompanied it. The author wrote that he had been a homosexual but had been made whole by God. He said that He had healed him.

Over the course of the next several weeks, we dug deep into the material. We had some great discussions, but we didn't always agree on everything.

One night, the minister said that he didn't believe gay people actually loved each other. I argued that I knew I had been in love with another man. He smiled as I spoke, but I didn't convince him based on my testimony or my belief. The lady who had been in a relationship with another woman seemed to side with my belief based on what she said during her testimony. Her facial expression matched the words that came out of her mouth that night.

I can confidently tell you that we were all being knit together in love. At least, I believe that's how I felt towards both of them. We were each struggling to find our healing, but we weren't alone. Each night, we ended the meeting by holding hands and praying for each other. Something happened inside of my heart when I heard the person next to me praying diligently to God on my behalf.

At our next meeting, we discussed the topic of idolatry. This was a tough night for me. It was hard to admit that I had made some of my boyfriends into idols that I ignorantly worshipped. I told you about my boyfriend that led to me telling my parents about being gay. I was trying to think about how I felt in that relationship. I agreed that I was willing to put my trust in him and that he would make me happy. I had come to the point where I was willing to sacrifice my family and my ministry for him (possibly even leaving God because I might have to choose between the two of them).

Let's press pause here on the meeting for a moment. I want to tell you more about what happened in my relationship with the man I thought was going to finally make me happy.

"Greg, I want to meet your boyfriend," my wife said.

"I don't think he would be open to meeting you, but I will ask him."

I rolled my eyes while thinking my wife had lost her mind. She is crazy to think he would be open to meeting her.

When I told him that my wife wanted to meet him, much to my surprise, he agreed to meet her. I was shocked and started to get scared about what might happen between the two of them when they met.

The moment of truth arrived. My wife greeted him at the entrance of our home. She introduced herself and asked him to have a seat at our kitchen table. She thanked him for agreeing to meet her. She started out by saying that she loved her husband very much. She went on to say that we had been through tough times together in our marriage and that she believed we would get through this challenge too.

"Greg loves God. He is very important to him. For that reason, I don't believe this relationship is going to last between the two of you."

By this time, he was getting uncomfortable with her confident declarations. He smiled politely as she tried to convince everyone in the room (maybe even God) about what she was saying.

I was silent on the outside, but I had a lot to say to myself on the inside. My heart hurt for her in that moment. I was stunned by her courage and faith.

Then, she asked us to please stand up.

"Let's join hands and pray," she said with a gentle but confident tone.

I was shocked again because my boyfriend reached out and took hold of her hand. I slowly reached out and took hold of both of their hands with mine. She prayed for our marriage, my ministry, and even for my boyfriend. It pierced my heart deeply. He and I left afterward to talk about what had just happened.

As my wife said, God was very important to me. I hadn't shared that side of myself with my boyfriend, but I had wanted to do so.

I asked my boyfriend to come and hear me preach at the church I was pastoring. My wife wasn't going to be able to be there on an upcoming Sunday morning. It would likely be one of the few times I'd have the opportunity to take him with me.

I introduced him to our church members as my friend. I was only half lying to them. This was kind of like in the Bible when Abraham told a king that Sarah was his sister instead of his wife. He was afraid the king would kill him in order to be with her because she was beautiful. I didn't think the congregation would have killed me, but I definitely believed that my ministry would have died that morning.

I was nervous that my boyfriend was with me in church for two reasons. One I mentioned already was about the members finding out the truth about me. The other was that God might not preach through me with him there.

My fears were quickly put to rest because the Holy Spirit stirred in me mightily that morning. I stepped down off the platform during my sermon.

"Jerusalem, Jerusalem, who kills the prophets and stones those who are sent to her! How often I wanted to gather your children together, the way a hen gathers her chicks under her wings, and you were unwilling,"

I said with an emotional tone that I don't ever remember using until that morning.

I felt these supernatural waves of compassion start rolling out of me. I don't know if anyone else felt them, but they were so strong that I struggled to remain standing on my feet. Anyone standing directly in front of me might have been knocked down by their power. My eyes were misted with tears because of the love of God I felt for everyone, including my boyfriend, who was sitting in the crowd. I will never forget this encounter with the Holy Spirit. I managed to somehow compose myself and finish the sermon.

My heart had been uncertain as to whether I believed God really hated people like me and my boyfriend. You have probably seen some signs that so-called Christians hold up at gay pride parades. After what I just told you, what do you believe?

Let's head back to the support group meeting and continue dealing with the subject of idolatry. Do you think my boyfriend was an idol to me after what I just shared with you? I was trying to hold onto God and my idol all at the same time. It really seems impossible looking back now. I wasn't only cheating on my wife with my boyfriend. I was cheating on God too. The apostle Paul writes about worshipping the creature more than the Creator in the opening chapter of Romans.

Eventually, our support group family decided to stop meeting. We tearfully prayed, thanking God for being with us during our times together. We had grown in this process. We asked God to keep our hopes alive.

"Yes, God, please never let my heart give up too soon. Maybe I might be delivered from my struggles someday? Only You know for sure," I whispered.

The minister seemed to have put homosexuality behind him. The lady and I had not. I will tell you that I have learned many more things about myself. My desires were still in conflict with what I believed the word of God said in the Bible, though.

13

I was a husband and a father despite how I felt about myself on the inside. I know I was far from being the kind of husband or father that I should have been. I had failed both my wife and sons way too many times. I am ashamed of that. I was so consumed with homosexuality that I was blind to what I was doing to all of them.

I can smile as I think about some of the times we had together as a family, though. We had lots of fun together. I am very thankful that we did. I will always cherish the memories that I have of those times.

One time, we went to a big amusement park. There was a very tall water slide. I climbed up and faced my fear of heights that day. I did it for my boys. I wanted them to see that you could face your fears.

When I got to the top, I wanted to turn around and climb back down.

What were you thinking? Are you really this crazy?

I wanted to go back down the way I came up.

No! You can do this. You need to do this for them.

After losing the argument that I was having with myself, I sat down on the platform. I slowly scooted my bottom up to the place where the water slide was connected. There was no railing on either side of the slide, so I could have easily fallen to my death if I hadn't lined up my body just right. I looked down and bravely waved to my sons, who were watching me. I shut my eyes and held my breath as I pushed off of the platform. It was an exhilarating rush that only lasted a few seconds. When I opened my eyes, I could see my sons were all smiles. They laughed at their dad as I struggled to get up because my swimming trunks had gone up my crack. I went back up and slid down a second time to make sure that I had conquered my fear. It ended the same way, with my sons smiling and my trunks in the same place. My fear of heights lost its grip on me that day.

My sons are amazing, like their mother. Growing up, they were two handsome boys (now, they are grown men with their own families). Both are very intelligent. One is more artistic, while the other is more athletic. One is very funny, but the other one has a sense of humor. The thing I admire most about both of them is that they have amazing hearts. They love their mother very much. She was the one who was always there for them growing up. I don't believe either one of them will ever forget that about her. Any father would be blessed to have them as sons, but God had entrusted them to me.

"God, please don't let either of my sons grow up to be like me!"

I desperately prayed this prayer to Him many times over the years they were growing up. My heart didn't want either of them to have to deal with homosexuality. My dealings had caused them and their mother more pain and disillusionment than anyone should ever have to endure.

One day, we were told that our youngest son may have had a rare kidney disease. We were fortunate that an intern at our family physician's office noticed that his eyes were puffy. He knew this mild swelling could possibly be a symptom of a kidney disease. After running a urinalysis, he recommended that we take him to have a biopsy done at a children's hospital in Nashville, Tennessee. His mother and I became very sober-minded. We soon learned, after the biopsy, that our son was in danger of losing his life for a second time. The first time was when he had a premature birth, which was due to my wife's declining health when she was eight months pregnant with him.

Once again, I was on my knees, asking for God to please save my son. We recruited as many prayer warriors as we could find among our family, our friends, and our church. The doctor prescribed some prednisone and a pill form of chemotherapy to treat our son's disease.

He swelled up dramatically with chipmunk cheeks to match the swelling in the rest of his body because of the steroids he had been prescribed to take. His classmates made fun of him. It broke my heart when I saw him crying about it. I knew what it felt like to be laughed at and made fun of for something you had no ability to control. His mother and I tried to console and comfort him the best way that we could. I wanted to take his pain and disease away. I didn't have the power to do so, but I knew Someone who did.

God answered another one of my prayers. He is so faithful! He healed my son of something that had a high probability of death. Only a small percentage of patients survive a disease as he had. A specialist in Louisville would later inform my wife that it was as if he never had the disease. We had experienced a miracle!

14

One night, I met another man in a gay bar. He was more handsome than anyone I had met up to this point. He had a smile that stopped me in my tracks. He had an innocence about him, but I would later learn that he wasn't as innocent as he looked. We went on a date shortly thereafter. We were riding in his car when it ran out of gas. He smiled sheepishly as we walked from the breakdown point to his apartment.

"I am sorry my car ran out of gas. You can take it out on me when we get back to my place."

"It's okay, but I'll be glad to oblige you when we get to your apartment," I said smilingly to let him know that I understood exactly what he wanted me to do.

My marriage began to struggle not too long after I had met this man. One night, my wife and I got into a fight. She knew about the man I was now in love with and told me to get out because of it. I don't know if she was totally serious or just blowing off steam. I was obedient to her command. I quickly left and headed over to my boyfriend's apartment.

I told him about what my wife had just said about me getting out.

"Why don't you move in with me?"

"Are you sure that's what you want?

He smiled and nodded his head to let me know that he did. I hugged and kissed him, thinking that maybe he was the one. He went with me back to my place so I could get some of my things. I was afraid that at any moment, he might change his mind, but I was more afraid of how my wife was going to react.

She looked extremely shocked and devastated all at the same

time as she watched me pack up some of my belongings. On another occasion, she had been angrily standing in our yard with her arms folded, watching my boyfriend and I drive away when he had picked me up for a date. Now, she'd have to watch me walk out the door, not knowing if I'd ever come back.

This time, for some reason, it was my turn to be angry. I used mine to give me the motivation I needed to move forward into a life that I believed was the only way I'd ever really be happy. I needed to face the fact that I was gay. Nothing or no one up to this point in my life had changed me, not even God.

I was embarking on an opportunity to try to be true to myself, possibly for the first time in my life. I tried to convince myself this was the best thing for everyone. I was tired of living a lie. I believed that my wife and kids would be better off without me.

At that time, I was working at a credit union. My co-workers may have suspected that I might be gay because my boyfriend was now driving me to work every morning. Often, he would drop off some breakfast for me through the drive-thru window. They were all nice to my face about my separation from my wife, but I didn't know what they might be saying behind my back. I didn't care because I felt like I was trying to be the person I really was. I was happy, but I wasn't ready to admit the truth to anyone outside of my family just yet.

My wife would later tell me that she prayed, believing that God would bring me back to her. She was a fighter. I drove my boyfriend's car to watch one of my son's baseball games. My wife confronted me in the parking lot in front of our kids, unfortunately. Apparently, she could see that I was unwavering in my determination to make my gay relationship work. It appeared as if I wasn't coming home anytime soon. She picked up a rock in her anger. Instead of throwing it at me, she used it to scratch the side of my boyfriend's car. I couldn't believe what I just witnessed. I angrily shook my head as I got into his car and slammed the door. I drove off in a fury. I knew how he felt about his car. It was his baby (even though it ran out of gas sometimes).

When I got back to my boyfriend's apartment, I had to confess about what my wife had just done. He was furious. I thought he might call it quits, but he didn't. I would later have another driver crash into the side of his car. It happened while I was backing out of a parking spot at the mall where he was working at the time. He just about lost his mind when that happened. Things began to start unraveling inside of him. I didn't have to be a prophet to see what may be looming in the near future.

Our relationship had started out great. We were romantic and happy in the beginning. At least, that's what it felt like to me. We rarely were apart except for when I was working at the credit union. He had gotten me a part-time job where he worked as a retail manager. I was able to work with him at night after I got off work at the credit union.

Now, we were drifting apart. It was more like I was on a raft, and he was on a speed boat. He was racing away from me. I didn't seem to have any way of going after him. I was forced to let the waves that his boat was making move me in the opposite direction.

He began falling asleep on the couch instead of coming to sleep with me in the bedroom. I became a neurotic mess. I believed that my happiness was asleep in the other room, and I couldn't wake him up.

Then, my birthday cake hit the fan. He was on the phone with his best friend. I had met her once, and I could tell she had feelings for him. I could tell he loved her, but in a platonic way. She had been there for him in some tough times. He seemed to have forgotten it was my birthday because he hadn't mentioned it. I grew angrier and angrier as I watched him smile and laugh with her on the phone.

After he hung up with her, I expressed that I was upset that he had forgotten my birthday. He blew up. He stormed over to the closet and flung open the door. He began to show me the gifts he had gotten me, along with the decorations he planned on hanging up to celebrate.

"I hope you like these because you aren't getting any of them! I am taking all of them back!" he yelled.

In a fury, he began to stuff them back into the store bags where he had purchased them. He slammed the door as he walked out and left me standing there all alone.

"What just happened?"

I tried to justify my emotions and jealousy, but the jury appeared to be on my boyfriend's side. Any love that he had ever felt for me was shoved into the same gift bags, and he was taking it back also.

All rise. The bailiff took the jury's decision and handed it to the judge. After reading it, he handed it back to the bailiff to read out loud to the courtroom. I staggered on the inside, trying not to crumble as I attempted to stand to my feet to hear the verdict. I held onto the chair for dear life. I knew what he was going to say before he ever uttered the words.

"We find the defendant guilty!"

"You need to gather up your stuff. You need to swallow your pride. Call your wife and beg her to forgive you. It's doubtful she will take you back!" the judge said as he slammed down his gavel.

Even though the judge said it was over, I wasn't one hundred percent convinced. I saved up enough money and bought him a bicycle that he had been wanting for his birthday. He was happy that I had gotten it for him, but it didn't have any power to make him love me again.

I decided to call it quits on our relationship. I couldn't take the rejection that I was feeling. He would storm off and leave without telling me where he was going. He would do this after starting a fight with me. I had all I could take. I needed to call my wife. I had to humble myself and tell her the truth.

"Maybe by some miracle, she will forgive me and take me back?" I said, hoping to myself.

I picked up the phone and called her.

"I want to come back home. I am so sorry I hurt you and our boys," I said, fighting back the tears.

"I have been waiting for this phone call. I am so happy that you want to come back. The boys and I will be waiting for you when you get here," she said with the most loving tone a dying man could ever hear.

I hung up the phone in disbelief.

Oh, I forgot to mention that she had given me a birthday present on my birthday. She is one amazing woman!

I looked my boyfriend straight in the eyes. I told him I was leaving and going back home. I began packing up my stuff without the slightest effort on his part to stop me. The only thing my ex-boyfriend seemed concerned about was the bicycle I had bought him for his birthday. He was afraid I was going to take back the gift that I had given him, just like he had done with mine. I left the bicycle and my shattered heart behind as I walked out of his life and into my uncertain future.

My wife and kids welcomed me back home. My boys were very happy that their daddy was back. It had been six months that I had lived apart from them. That night, I cried in the arms of my wife, releasing a lot of shame and regret for how deeply I had hurt her. It was one of the most healing and powerful moments where I was able to be vulnerable with her. She was amazingly loving and supportive to me.

"How can this be? How can she still love me and want me to be her husband? This makes no earthly sense to me. God, thank You for giving me a family that I don't deserve. Thank You for not abandoning me when You had every right to do so. What kind of love is this? I don't understand how You could still want me either? Somehow, though, I believe that You do."

He didn't answer me, but I don't think my eyes were the only ones with tears in them.

Let me ask you a question: knowing what you've heard so far, would you still love me if you were married to me? If you were me, would you still love yourself? And what about God? Do you think He could really love me after what I've told you so far? Can you understand how I thought I would end up being unwanted by the people in my life? By God?

Well, I'd like to say the worst of my story is over, but there is still much I need to share with you. I pray that you keep reading. Hold on because there are a lot more climbs and falls to go until we get to the end.

15

If you recall, back in the beginning of my story, I told you that my singing in church was apparently awful, but I couldn't stop singing. Well, let me take you back to some of the times in my life when I had been blessed and hurt because of my singing.

When I was a young boy, I would sing all the time. Often, I sang for my grandmother and aunt. They seemed to like it, or at least they tolerated me doing it with a smile on their faces.

When I was in the fourth grade, my teacher impacted my life in a profound way. She began to encourage me and to brag about me to the other students in my class. I would wind up going from making average grades to good ones over time because of her influence and encouragement.

One day, our class had a day of show-and-tell. She instructed us to go up and share something in front of the class. I didn't have a clue what I was going to present.

One of the boys in my class sang for everyone. I decided I would sing for my turn also. I was very nervous, but I sang anyway. I chose a song from one of the Saturday morning kids shows that I liked.

After I finished, the teacher jumped to her feet, clapping and beaming. I wish everyone could be as blessed as I was to have a teacher like her. What a profound impact she made in my life.

She asked me to sing the next morning, but I opted out for some reason. Maybe it was because I did not know the words to many songs all the way through? Or maybe stage fright got the best of me that morning? To be honest, I am not exactly sure why I declined her offer.

When I was in junior high school, I auditioned for the choir. The music teacher's expression afterward let me know that I had just bombed. Whatever I had in the fourth grade had left my voice somewhere along the way. She had mercy on me and let me join the choir anyway. I was happy, but any confidence I had in singing was gone.

One of my older brothers laughed at me whenever he heard me singing. He thought I couldn't sing, and he told me so. He said that it sounded like I was singing through my nose when I tried.

The church where I preached my first sermon had a choir. I loved our song leader and his wife (she played the piano). He knew how much I loved music and that I wanted to sing so badly.

One day in choir practice, he had me sing the verses of a song. He asked the choir to sing the choruses with me. I was so excited to get the opportunity. Not long into the rehearsal, one of the deacons stormed out of the choir with a look on his face that I will never forget. It was easy to see that he was upset that his brother (the song leader) was even giving me a chance to sing this song. He thought it was ridiculous to let someone try to sing when they couldn't. That might have been a misperception on my part, but I don't think that I was wrong in what I believed.

My heart was embarrassed and broken. The song leader tried to encourage me to keep singing with a look that suggested I forget about what just happened. I wished I could have, but I just couldn't.

I went to the altar that night at our church at the end of the service. I cried out to God while my heart was drowning in immense pain and sorrow. I hoped that God would somehow come to my rescue because I didn't think that I was going to survive this rejection by one of the leaders in our church. When the deacon saw how much pain I was in, he tried to say he was sorry. I accepted his apology, but the damage he caused was going to take some time to heal, if ever.

Let's leave me in the pain and suffering that singing had caused me. There's a lot more for me to tell you about it.

Is it just me, or am I not the only one who doesn't understand why the things we seem to want the most are the hardest ones to achieve?

16

"Greg, I talked to a television talk show producer today. I told him I had seen a show recently where some women had found out about their husband's homosexuality. It destroyed their marriages. I told him that I loved you despite your homosexuality. I went on to say that we have a good marriage. They want us to appear on an upcoming show. Isn't that great?" my wife asked.

"You've got to be kidding me?"

"No, I am not kidding! They will need to talk to you before we go on the show."

I could see she was telling me the truth. She watched my face closely to see if there might be any chance of talking me into doing this.

Going on the show would almost be like committing relational suicide because I thought most people would turn their backs on me once they knew the truth. Plus, I believed I would be killing any chance I'd have to ever preach again.

On the other hand, I thought about other married men who could be going through some of the same stuff that I was.

"Maybe it would be a good thing to go on the show? It might give some of them the courage to talk about their own struggles?" I said, trying to talk myself into doing what my wife wanted to do.

She seemed adamant about wanting us to appear on the show. I had put her through so much. I could at least give her something that she wanted for a change.

Up to this point, I had only talked openly about my homosexuality with some of my family members. I know that the people at the credit union where I worked must have figured out that I had been living with another man (not just as roommates) during my six-month separation. Looking back, I don't remember talking openly with any of them.

Where was I going to find the courage to tell my secret on national television? How did I let my wife and myself talk me into doing this thing? Are you crazy? I asked myself.

I must have lost my mind, or hopefully, it was only temporary insanity!

I was terrified for people to find out the truth. It is one thing to have people suspect something, but to hear it come out of your mouth is quite another. Do you remember how my parents reacted when I told them the truth (even though my wife told them ahead of time)?

I was just so tired of letting people down and/or hurting them. The damage I had done to my wife is unforgivable in most people's books, including mine. My secrets were about to step onto a dark stage and have a bright spotlight shined down on them while they uncovered themselves.

I had never flown in an airplane. My fears and I were buckled in for takeoff. My wife was holding my hand, trying to calm both of us down. I don't know which I was more scared of, dying in a plane crash or crashing my own life into the ground. The truth was about to explode on impact while the whole world watched in horror.

The plane's engines revved up, and so did my stomach. I squeezed my wife's hand and shut my eyes while managing to shoot a prayer up into the sky to God. As the plane lifted off the ground, I hoped that my prayer had likewise. Once we were up in the air, my nerves seemed to calm down. It would be a short-lived break in anxiety.

Our plane landed safely in New York City. The buildings were much taller and more intimidating in person than they appeared in pictures or on television. We had a driver waiting for us at the airport. He took us to the nice hotel that the talk show had booked for us. We were not being paid to appear on the show, but they covered all of our travel expenses.

"Thank God for the Gideons!"

They had left a Bible in the hotel room. It was hiding in the nightstand beside the bed. I searched through the pages until I found this passage.

"For nothing is hidden that will not become evident, nor anything secret that will not be known and come to light" (Luke 8:17, NASB).

Jesus made this proclamation. Luke recorded it for us. He also wrote down the following statement that Jesus made.

"But there is nothing covered up that will not be revealed, and hidden that will not be known. Accordingly, whatever you have said in the dark will be heard in the light, and what you have whispered in the inner rooms will be proclaimed upon the housetops."

Well, if that's true (and I believed it was), at least my secret would be told on my terms, I thought.

Little did I know, it would be anything but on my terms.

My wife and I were sitting in the green room, waiting to be escorted out into the studio to appear on the show. It should have been obvious to anyone in that room that I was on the verge of a nervous breakdown. The show had hired a psychologist who was appearing on the show with us. She was there waiting with us, along with the other two couples who would be telling their secrets (Family Secrets was the topic of the show). She came over and asked if she could sit down next to me.

"Are you alright? You look very nervous and upset."

"I am not okay. I have only confessed my secret about being gay to a few people in my family. To come out of the closet on national television is probably not the best advice I'd give anyone, especially myself!" I replied while wiping the sweat off my hands onto my pants.

"Since the show airs during the day, I doubt if many people will even see the show because most will be at work," she responded back in a warm tone, which managed to ease my nerves a little bit.

I had heard of people being talked down off a ledge before, but I had never heard of someone being encouraged into getting up onto a ledge and then being cheered on to jump off. But here I was, probably the first one to ever have that happened to them.

One of the producers who was standing nearby overheard our conversation. He said that I could wear a disguise if necessary. Some of the other guests had chosen to wear one in order to hide their faces.

I climbed out on the ledge, trying not to look down while convincing myself that I was about to jump off for my wife and some of the men who might tune in. I wasn't about to hide behind some mask, so I let it fall to the ground before I jumped.

We were escorted to our seats on the stage. One of the staff members put microphones on each of us. We were instructed that we must try not to cough because the sound would be amplified for all to hear.

Choking, not coughing, seemed like a much more appropriate word. I had a tie on, but that wasn't the reason for the tightening I felt in my throat. We were sitting before a crowd of people who were about to judge me.

The talk show host came out to the excitement of the audience. They were obediently applauding because the applause sign was lit. One of the producers had given them instructions to please do so when they saw the sign light up. I believe I was the only one in the room who wasn't clapping.

The host began questioning my wife about our story. She told him that I was gay and that she loved me. Then, to my surprise, he asked about the relationship where I had left her for six months. How did he know this information? Because I didn't tell any of the producers.

Before we go on with the show, I need to let you know that one of my ex-boyfriend's workmates threw him a birthday party and invited me. It was difficult seeing him again, but I kept my composure. There was a very good-looking guy at the party. He and my ex seemed to have a mutual attraction. I watched as they made flirtatious advances and kept smiling at each other throughout the night. Later, this guy asked me if I still had feelings for my ex. I told him he should pursue him if he was interested without answering his question.

Much to my surprise, my ex got very drunk and started coming on to me. I was somewhat intoxicated too. I didn't fight off his advances.

After everyone had left his apartment, we wound up in his bedroom. I passed out afterward. I woke up the next morning to the sound of someone pounding on his apartment door. He went to the door to see who it was. I recognized my wife's voice when she asked him where I was. He tried to stop her from going any further into his apartment. I wasn't about to get out of his bed to see what I could easily hear was happening between them. She came storming into his bedroom. There was a pain in her eyes that was hard for me to look at. It was as if she was emotionally hanging from the end of an invisible rope. She put her hands on her hips. Then, she looked me straight in the eyes to make sure I knew how serious she was.

"Greg, I can't do this anymore. I love you. I want to stay married to you, but you have to make a choice. Is it going to be me or him?" she demanded.

I knew I had to decide right then and there.

"I am sorry. I will get dressed and come home."

She left. I put my clothes on and told him goodbye.

"Well, I took another swing at him, and then I went to get my husband!" my wife said to the talk show host as the crowd roared with laughter.

She was telling them about what I just shared with you. It felt like they were all laughing at me.

My wife was not only beautiful (some of the staff told her she looked like Delta Burke on camera), but she was very funny and animated, just like Delta. She was at the top of her abilities at that moment. Her facial expressions were telling everyone even more than her words could convey. She didn't seem the least bit afraid to talk about her past.

Looking back, I believe humor is what she used to cope with all the pain she had been through in her life. Her parents divorced early in her life, and she never seemed to recover from it. Her father remarried and moved away out of state. He wasn't the father she wanted or needed him to be.

Her husband was no different than her dad. Both men seem to have caused her to feel unwanted way too many times. I believe she tried to laugh it off instead of crumbling under the weight of the disappointments and heartaches that threatened to crush her. That's just my observation. She might argue otherwise.

Now, the host turned his attention to me.

I was warned by one of the producers not to talk too much about God or the Bible. He said it would turn people off. I didn't heed his words completely.

I had read a book on homosexual desires conflicting with what God says in His Word. The author had been gay in the past. He claimed that he had been *delivered* by God from his unwanted same-sex attractions. I had tried to convince myself that I wasn't gay anymore like the author had said in his book. I understood analytically what I had read. My heart was far away from my head, but I didn't know it at the time. I will explain more about this later. I tried to articulate to the host what I had learned from this book. I failed miserably. This is mostly what came out of my mouth.

"The Bible says it's wrong to be gay. I don't think I am actually gay anymore."

The host smiled, but he didn't believe any part of it.

"I don't believe you can pray and ask God to change you from being gay into straight," he said very convincingly.

I wondered if he might be right about what he was saying because he seemed very sure of himself. He then turned his attention to the fact that my wife and I were holding hands. He jokingly said that it appeared as if my wife had ahold of me.

"She has him by the hand, and she's not letting go anytime too soon!" he said as the crowd erupted in laughter once again.

"That's right," my wife said smilingly as she agreed with him that she wasn't.

Shame began flooding into my soul. It felt as if there were demons in the audience laughing at me too. After the show, the host shook my hand.

"I hope you're not mad at me?"

I assured him that I wasn't mad at him, but I was infuriated at myself!

What just happened? How stupid and gullible can you be to not see something like this coming? I thought.

On the plane ride back home, I didn't pray for a safe landing. I was mentally and emotionally exhausted. I could have cared less if we crashed. I feared that my life was about to come crashing down all around me. I believed I was going to be an outcast in our community once the show aired. I tried to find some hope in what the psychologist told me before going on the show. Remember when she said she didn't think that many people would watch the show? I could only pray she was right.

She wasn't right. Our local newspaper ran an article announcing that we were going to be on the show and what it was all about. One of the show's producers had called the paper and told them that they were going to be airing the program in the very near future. Dread filled my heart because anyone could set their VCRs to record it while they were at work.

I was standing in my boss's office at the credit union where I worked.

"I don't think I would have the balls to be on a show and tell everyone my secrets," he said to me with an incredulous look on his face.

I took in a deep breath before I responded to him.

"I thought it would help some others who might be in my same situation."

"That's admirable, but there's no way I would or could have done what you did."

Let's pause here because I need to tell you about another boyfriend I had sometime after the one I had moved in with for six months when I left my wife. This relationship was more like a fling.

After I broke off our relationship, he tried to get even with me for breaking his heart. He sent a letter to the credit union telling them that I had done drag and had stripped at a local gay bar in town. When my bosses confronted me, I lied and said it wasn't true.

I had only done one drag show. It was a fluke. My friend had dressed me up in some of his drag clothes and had taken me with him to the bar. Lots of people told me they thought I looked good. They asked me to do a song on stage. After downing a few drinks, I accepted their offer. I liked the attention that I received that night. I even thought I looked good. However, I didn't like the makeup, the dress, the wig, the brazier, the pantyhose, or the high heels that it took to make me look the way I did. As far as I can remember, I never dressed up in drag again.

Another night, the gay bar was having an all-male strip show. I jokingly said to one of the bartenders that I would strip if the dancers didn't show up. Only one guy showed up. The owner had overheard my earlier conversation, and so he asked me if I would dance out of his desperation to still have the show. He offered me one hundred dollars plus the tips I would make. Again, after drinking a couple of shots, I reluctantly said yes.

I had another drink before I went backstage. I didn't have anything to wear. The dancer who had shown up let me borrow one of his G-strings.

I stood behind the curtain, hoping that maybe it wouldn't open. I was very nervous about stripping down to almost nothing in front of a crowd. I took a deep breath as I stepped out onto the stage. I was immediately blinded by the spotlight. I squinted as I tried to dance to an unrehearsed routine. The crowd began encouraging me to take off what I was wearing. In the end, I liked the attention, but I didn't like wearing a G-string.

In both scenarios, the gay community didn't reject me. I dressed up like a woman, and they cheered. I danced almost naked before them, and they cheered.

I did a few more strip shows at the local gay bar. I even did one at a bachelorette party. I did not like the way I started feeling about myself after I had taken off my clothes. I ended my dancing career. It was very short-lived.

By the time the letter was sent, I wasn't stripping or doing drag. So, I said the letter wasn't true. I don't think they believed that I was telling the truth. One manager said he wasn't about to start trying to follow all of his employees around outside of work to see what they were doing.

After the show aired, the credit union received a few complaint calls. Our human resources director told the callers that I was a good employee. She told them what I did in my personal life wasn't the management's job to judge or to hold me accountable.

Much to my surprise, most of my friends didn't treat me differently than before they knew the truth about me. My fear that most people would reject me was put to rest. Hopefully, it would stay buried and never rise again.

Unfortunately, my desires began to resurface yet again. I resisted them as long as I could before I went back out to try and quench them. I was standing in a gay bar in my hometown when a guy came up and got in my face.

"What are you doing in here? (he recognized me from the talk show). I hated you for going on that show and saying you weren't gay anymore! How could you do that?" he asked with disdain on his face and disgust in his eyes.

I unsuccessfully tried to explain that I was confused when I went on the show. I said I mainly did it because my wife wanted me to do it. He shook his head angrily as he walked away in disbelief. If you know anything about the creation story in Genesis, I had acted just like Adam, who blamed his wife (Eve) when he was confronted by God after he ate from the forbidden tree of the knowledge of good and evil.

Now, I was feeling unwanted because of someone in the gay community. It could easily look as if I had turned my back on them by appearing on the show. I had met many of them who had been hurt in the past. Some had been rejected by many in the world, the church, and even by some of their own families. This community had fought to find acceptance and love, just like I had been desperately searching for most of my life. I was left there standing alone. I began feeling more guilt and shame.

17

I applied for the head teller position at the credit union branch where I was working. The manager interviewed me for the position and was about to promote me. For some reason, he decided to ask my fellow coworkers about me at the branch where I was working. I often ran the drive-thru window at the branch. I had an ability to not only remember the members' names but also many of their account numbers. They would always get a kick out of my knowing who they were and their account numbers.

I was sitting in the manager's office as he told me I wasn't getting promoted. It seemed I had been stabbed in the back by some of the ladies I worked with. The knife they used was now sticking in my heart, where it was causing me some deep, unwanted pain. I was not sure I managed to hide the fact that I was deeply wounded because of this betrayal. I went home and cried in the arms of my wife. She tried to console me as I sobbed, saying I didn't understand why they would lie about me. I tried to believe that maybe God had something different in mind for me. I understood at that moment how He possibly might have felt in the garden of Gethsemane when Judas gave him a kiss of betrayal. My hope of being promoted had been "crucified" due to some lies my coworkers told. I thought they were my friends, but I guess I was wrong.

Sometime later, I got promoted to our financial planning department at the credit union. My position was to be an assistant to the financial planner. My new boss was a very difficult man to work for, I must say. He had already gone through several other assistants that I had seen come and go not long after they started. All of them were women. This man and the branch manager had approached me asking if I would consider this position. I ignored the red flags I saw and accepted the job. I would become the only one who somehow managed to persevere (miraculously) working for him. It required me almost biting my tongue off on many occasions and resisting the temptation to walk out. Often, he made belittling and snide remarks that would hurt and anger me.

After our first year together, my boss gave me a review. He told me that I handled adversity unlike anyone he'd ever met before.

"I don't know how you do it. Is it that you just don't give a crap or what?"

"I have learned how to lean on God in the most difficult times in my life. He has strengthened me and helped me when I didn't think I was going to make it through them."

He shook his head in amazement because he had witnessed some of my difficulties, including the separation between me and my wife.

I learned that my boss's position had been vacated at another credit union in Louisville, Kentucky. I decided to apply for this position. I felt like it would be a long shot to get this job. I had been successful in helping my current boss increase sales, and I also had conducted a few seminars for him and with him.

The very first seminar I conducted was without him. I presented some financial planning strategies dealing with retirement plans to some employees at one of the largest companies in our town. At the end of the presentation, the employees clapped. The woman who asked us to come and present told me after everyone had left that no presenter before me had ever received any applause. I was excited because that was confirmation to me that I had done what I was sent there to do. I excitedly told my boss what she had said. He shot down my enthusiasm by saying he didn't need the "clap" to give him any affirmation. It hurt me deeply, but I think my face had let him know how he made me feel.

I loved playing competitive volleyball. Over time, I advanced my skills to a fairly high level. Louisville was a much larger town than where I currently lived. Volleyball was very popular there. With a lot more people playing, I would have the opportunity to play in the many leagues and tournaments that were hosted in various spots around the city. My moving there would not only be a great career opportunity, but I would be blessed to be able to play against players who were at a higher level than I was on a regular basis. Hopefully, it would propel me into becoming an even better player in the sport that I had grown to love.

I was chosen by my boss's boss to fill the open position. I wasn't full of any anxiety (just excitement) because I was familiar with the place I was moving to. I had met a lot of the volleyball players in some of the Louisville tournaments I had already competed in, plus I had played with a traveling USVBA team from there too.

My volleyball career would consist of me winning some of the tournaments I would later play in this amazing city. The various leagues and tournaments I would eventually compete in were indoor sixes, grass triples, sand doubles, and sand quads.

I wanted to tell you about playing volleyball because it gave me an opportunity to get to know some of the kind of guys whom I had been intimidated by in the past. Most of these men appeared to be masculine and seemed to be comfortable in their own skin. I tried to stay at a distance from these kinds of guys for fear of hearing them call me a sissy or a fag, like when I was a boy. Before I knew it, I began to let my guard down.

To my surprise, I would come to find out that they were not that different from me. I had believed a lie about them. In fact, I grew to love many of these players, not in a homosexual kind of way (although I was attracted to some of them), but as a friend and like a brother. We hung out on and off the volleyball courts. I made friends with some of the women who played the sport too. I hope that any preconceived notions they may have had about me being gay might have changed once they got close enough to learn the truth about who I really was.

I moved to Louisville without my wife and sons. She had tried to find another job in Louisville but was unsuccessful. Financially, we couldn't make it on just my income, so she continued working in her current job until she could find one in Louisville. I was restless with all the free time that I had, so I began going out a lot of nights to some gay bars in town.

One night, a handsome man caught my eye. My attraction immediately compelled me to walk over to where he was playing pool so I could get a closer look. His shirt was unbuttoned, revealing his chiseled pectorals. He laughed at his opponent after he missed an easy shot. His smile was warm, and it rivaled almost any that I'd ever seen. When he finally looked at me, he flashed it again. I smiled back at him. He came over and struck up a conversation with me after his game ended. We would end up going back to his place.

I woke up lying next to him in his bed the next morning. I had felt more than just a physical transaction had taken place. I was hoping that I wasn't the only one who had felt it. He woke up only wearing the smile he had on the night before.

Immediately, my heart began to hope again. Maybe this is the guy I had been looking for? I'd had a couple of serious relationships in my past, but they had ended differently than I had wanted. I had resigned myself to having anonymous sexual encounters that ended without me usually spending the night or even cuddling with them afterward. However, this one ended with me searching for my clothes on his floor, but I believed I just found someone to love.

"I want to see you again," he said, with that smile I found irresistible.

"I want to see you again too," I said, hoping that he couldn't overhear the excitement that my heart was feeling.

I didn't want to scare him away before we even got the chance to fall in love. I didn't want to let go of his embrace as I kissed him goodbye.

It didn't take me long to find my way back to his place. With my wife living out of town, we were able to spend most of our free time together. I was falling again for another guy, but this one was different than any of my other boyfriends. We enjoyed lifting weights together at his gym. He would come and watch me play volleyball. We were interested in each other beyond the passion we were experiencing in the bedroom. It didn't take too long before my wife found out about him.

"I think you should stay where you are. You love your job. The boys won't have to be pulled out of their schools or taken away from their friends," I said to my wife.

"Greg, I love you, and nothing is going to change that. I know you think you love this man you want to be with, but you know it's not God's will for you. It won't last," my wife said, refusing to be convinced by my reasons for her to stay away.

"I guess you are going to do what you are going to do, and so am I. I am not going to quit seeing him," I replied while being frustrated at her unrelenting resolve.

Are you amazed as much as I was? As I write this book, it's been very hard for me to look at how many times I hurt her. Somehow, she would continue pursuing me with her love. It makes no earthly sense to me still today. God must have been giving my wife this supernatural ability (grace) because I'd never seen it in anyone like this before. The Bible says His mercies are new every morning (Lamentations 3:23). Apparently, my wife had the same kind of heart as God does. I didn't deserve for either of them to love me, but I certainly felt it from both of them.

I was a narcissist who was pursuing his own happiness while leaving my wife behind to suffer in her loneliness and despair. I was blind back then, but now I see how ugly I had become in my quest to make myself happy.

This next part is very hard for me to tell you. I believe it will be equally hard for you to read. God is watching over all those who fear Him. He rescued someone I loved, but I was unwilling to believe it. It would be during one of the darkest times of her life. Even though I had left her alone, God was with her.

I got a phone call from one of my wife's dearest friends. This woman informed me that she had taken some pills in hopes of taking her own life.

"She is okay, but she is very shook up by what just happened. The ER doctor pumped her stomach. Someone found her on the floor and called 911," her friend said.

I thanked her for letting me know before I ended the call.

I must tell you that I wasn't feeling compassion. I thought she staged this act to get my attention. Where compassion normally should have been, I had anger instead. If memory serves me correctly, she had taken the pills at her workplace.

How could she have risked her life by doing this? There were no guarantees she would be found by someone in time. How could she risk leaving her sons without a mother? I thought to myself.

A doctor would later get in my face and tell me that my wife was desperately crying out. He said, "You need to be there for her regardless of how you feel about what she did or who you might be in love with."

My wife would later tell me that she was in so much pain and hopelessness that she just couldn't find a reason to live anymore. I had believed another lie. I had made it all about me instead of seeing the devastation I had caused her.

My wife finally found a job in Louisville. She left her suicidal tendencies behind her as she moved forward with hopes of starting over in a new city. She and my sons moved into my apartment while I moved out of it.

My boyfriend was renting a room at a house owned by two guys who were lovers. At first, they welcomed me into their home, but it very quickly became too crowded. They asked him (us) to move out.

We ended up moving in with my lover's mom until we could find a place of our own. She told me she loved her son very much.

"I know he's looking for someone to love him," she said when it was just her and I standing alone together in her living room.

"I love your son," I said, trying to convince her that I might be the one her son had been looking for most of his gay life.

She looked into my eyes, searching for the truth because she had seen other men come and go in his life.

I became very uncomfortable living in her home with the two of them. She reminded me of my mother by the way she tried to control her son. Let's just say that she wasn't the only one trying. He was stuck in the middle of both of us, trying to dominate his will. I grew up watching my mother control my father and trying to control me too. I didn't like being dominated by her. Now, here I was doing the same thing to someone I loved. I couldn't seem to stop myself. He was very sweet and compliant to the neurotic demands I had forced on him. Often, he had to reassure me that he loved me and that he had no intentions of ever cheating on me.

We began searching for an apartment together. He knew from the conversations we had had that I was not happy with our current living arrangements. I persuaded him to look for a place in the redneck part of Louisville instead of one in a gay-friendly neighborhood. I told him that I believed that would be a wise choice in order to protect our relationship from any outside threats of destruction. He reluctantly accepted my idea. He believed that while we may be protecting ourselves from being tempted to cheat, some redneck might be tempted to bash us in the head.

We found an apartment in an area where I thought our relationship could survive. My neurotic tendencies eased up a little, and I began to settle into our new home.

Shortly thereafter, God began drawing me back to Himself.

There was a church just up the road from where we were living. I asked my boyfriend if he would go there with me some Sunday morning to see what the church was like.

"I will go with you, but if they preach about homosexuality or say that it is a sin, I won't go back."

I smiled as I tried to assure him that I doubted they would do such a thing.

What are the odds of something like this happening?

The very next Sunday morning, we were in this particular church, sitting on one of their pews. The preacher started out the service, holding up a flyer. He announced that there was an upcoming event where the topic of homosexuality was going to be discussed. This man said that he believed that it was a sin that God condemned in the Bible. My boyfriend looked at me with an "I told you so" expression. He began to try and ignore what was being said right in front of his face. It was anything but good news to him. He turned his face away towards the wall, trying not to look at me or the man he thought was spewing hate speech. I don't know which one of us he was the angriest at. It was either the preacher, me or himself. Probably me because I had persuaded him into going, even though it was against his will to be there. When he turned his face back towards me, I turned mine towards him. His eyes told me everything he wanted me to know. No words were necessary. He wasn't ever going back to church with me again.

I was puzzled as to the timing of us attending this church the very day the preacher would be speaking out against homosexuality.

"God, I don't understand. My heart is breaking for him right now because I know that he doesn't know You," I prayed.

I remembered a discussion I had with him and a couple of his gay friends. I had been talking about God with them. I had shared about how I loved Him and how I had felt loved back by Him. One of his friends looked at me with this deep pain in his eyes.

"Do you know how many gay men would give anything to have this same kind of close relationship that you have with God?" he asked.

I tried to convince him and the others standing there that they could have a similar relationship with Him, but I don't think they believed me. I shook my head as I prayed inwardly to God to please help all of them to find what I had found with Him.

Now, my hope of my boyfriend having a relationship with God was left sitting on a pew as I watched him storm out of the church in a rage. I got up and followed after him. I caught up close enough to him to hear his truck door slam shut after he got in. I slowly got in on the passenger side. As he started up the engine, he looked at me with a mix of pain and anger.

"I am never coming back here again," he shouted, confirming what I already knew in my heart.

I sadly agreed to never ask him to go with me again.

I continued pursuing God by myself. I began to see that when I was in a loving relationship with a man, my restlessness would leave, and I would pursue God again. When I wasn't in a close relationship with a man, I would drift from God and embark on some quest to find happiness that never seemed to last very long.

Once again, I became conflicted, just like I did in the past. The double bind that one of my counselors told me about was back again. I was faced with another decision to make. I was trying to convince myself that I could love God while being in a sinful relationship with this man that I loved. John wrote that Jesus said if you love me, keep my commandments.

I was sitting in our living room on the couch with my boyfriend. There was some space between us, which allowed us to look into each other's eyes. Tears were welling up in mine as I told him that I loved him, but that I couldn't be there with him anymore. I told him that a war had just ended between my conscience and my heart regarding our relationship. I said, unfortunately, my heart lost the battle and that I was going to move out. I didn't tell him that I could feel some cracks beginning to form in my heart due to the violent earthquake that was shaking it at that very moment. The unwanted news he was being told was unexpected, and he was starting to cry too.

Then, the Holy Spirit's presence filled the room where we were sitting. I am not sure if he could feel Him, but he may have because of what came out of his mouth next. It was anything but what I expected to hear him say to me.

"I feel like I am talking to an angel right now," he said while wiping away his tears.

"I am definitely not an angel," I objected.

Somehow, I was able to stand to my feet, and I kissed him goodbye.

I cried all the way back to my wife's apartment building. The reason for leaving my boyfriend in our old hometown was because of how he had treated me. This time, I left my current boyfriend because of God and the conviction I felt.

My wife was very happy to see that I had come back to her and our sons. I had been away from them for another six-month period. My wife said that she and the boys needed to go somewhere but would be back shortly.

"Are you going to be okay while I am gone?' she asked because she could tell that I was very upset.

"I think I will be okay," I said, trying to convince myself more than I was trying to convince her.

My wife and kids left.

The sound of the door closing behind them was all that was needed to set off an aftershock of the emotional earthquake that had just occurred earlier that day. My heart began shattering apart as the shock waves of pain went through it. My legs gave way to my body, collapsing down onto the floor in the bedroom. I pulled my knees into my chest as I prayed to try to survive this unwanted attack. To say I was undone is an understatement!

"How will I ever survive this? I don't ever want to feel this way again," I told myself.

I had only felt this kind of helplessness one other time in my life.

It was when I watched my mother, who was dying while she laid on the couch in my parent's home. She was gasping for air as she labored to take another breath into her diseased lungs. Hospice was there to help her pass as comfortably as possible.

Almost six years earlier, our family doctor broke the bad news to us that my mom had one of the most aggressive breast cancers. With tears in his eyes, he said that she was in the fight of her life. He had grown to love my mother and our family. He had helped her deliver some of her babies into the world. He had been there in some of the happiest moments of our lives.

My father, my four siblings, and I gathered all around her as she took her last breath while we were holding ours. It was the most difficult moment of my life, where I had to witness the one person whom I loved more than most struggling to stay alive. There's nothing you can do but pray to the One who can do something that you cannot.

Her spirit left her body to be with our Heavenly Father as I tried to comfort my earthly father, who had just lost the love of his life. We were all experiencing a loss that was shaking us apart. We'd weathered storms together in the past, but the glue that had held us together during those times was gone.

The thought of losing my mother was one of my two greatest fears. The other was people finding out about my homosexuality. God met me in the most profound way the very moment she left to be with Him. I wish I could describe to you the way the Holy Spirit ministered to my heart. Even now, I don't know how to tell you how He did it. I was able to grieve losing her without falling apart. It was hard to see her lying in the funeral home awaiting her burial, but it wasn't like I feared it would be. I knew it wouldn't be the last time I'd ever see her again. Her body was lying there, but her soul had gone to be with her God, who had given her eternal life.

Do you remember when I told you about my relationship with my mother not being what I thought it was? I believed our relationship had been based on her terms and her will, without me having a say in it.

God told me that my relationship with Him wasn't what I thought it was, either. That was a tough thing to hear, but I needed to hear it. He said He wasn't free to tell me what He wanted to tell me about regarding His dreams and His will for my life. He said I would be obedient to some of the things He asked me to do until I got mad when the outcome didn't turn out the way I expected (my will, not His be done). He said sometimes I didn't listen to Him at all. I will tell you a lot more about our conversations throughout my story. I am so glad He has been faithful when I wasn't. He comforted me in a way I will never forget when my mom died. I could never repay Him for the loving kindness He has shown to me.

Back to my bedroom, where I was lying on the floor in a fetal position, crying like a baby. I cried out because of the pain I was in, but I also began to cry out to God.

"Please help me. I know I am the last person who deserves Your help. I am trying to do what your Word says. Please have mercy on me!" I prayed.

He answered by letting me know He was with me. Sometimes, you just need someone to be with you in your despair. They don't have to say a word. Just knowing they are with you is enough.

I want to tell you that even though I wanted to do the right thing, I often had difficulty pulling it off. I wound up going back and falling into bed with the guy who thought I might be an angel. I guess that belief probably left his heart when I showed back up on his doorstep.

"Please stay away if it's really over. It's just too hard for me to keep doing this," he said.

I could see what I was doing to him, so I didn't go back anymore.

My wife and I began getting closer again. How can she still love me knowing what I've done? My questions may never get answered as to how she was able to forgive me after I kept devastating her way too many times to count. There is no rhyme or reason for this, is there?

"God, how can You love me, knowing what I've done? I don't understand why I am still alive. Why haven't You destroyed me yet? Why did you ever call me to preach, knowing I was attracted to men?" I prayed with hot tears rolling down my anguished face.

He didn't answer me, but I felt His presence.

18

I continued reading every new Christian book that came out about the subject of homosexuality. My wife found many of these books for me at Christian bookstores. There were various books dealing with psychology, inner healing, damaged relationships with parents, sexual abuse, as well as other factors that the authors believed caused men and women to become gay. One author believed that reparative therapy could heal the man who was indecisive about his attraction to other men.

I was always happy to get the opportunity to read another book on my dilemma. I always hoped that maybe it would be the one that unlocked the healing that I wanted at that time. After reading all these books, I had a lot of head knowledge, but it didn't change my heart's desire for men.

I began attending a support group for gay men who wanted to change their sexual orientations. We met weekly at a church in Louisville.

The meetings were a great place to share a lot of what was going on internally, relationally, and spiritually in our lives. There were both married and single guys who came with the hope of changing. The counselor who led the group was a very kind and compassionate man. He never struggled with same-sex attraction, but he understood some of the theories on the subject.

One of the challenges that occurred was that it was no secret why each of us was there. What would we do if one of the men in our group finds themself attracted to someone else in our group? We would have to work out this issue if it happened (and it did), as well as some of our immature relational skills too.

We started praying for each other at the end of our sessions. We cheered each other on as we fought for sexual sobriety. We became brothers in the Lord on our quest to find our identity in the One who had created us.

During this time, I had a job at a small mortgage company in Louisville. One of my bosses missed work one morning with a stomach virus.

The next morning, I woke up in bed with stomach pains. I immediately thought the pains were from a virus I may have caught in the office. I rushed to the bathroom because I thought I was going to throw up. The pain was starting to become violent. I had never experienced anything like what I was feeling abdominally. By the time I reached the bathroom, I vomited, but the pain didn't subside. My diaphragm kept trying to get my stomach to cooperate by expelling anything else that might bring my discomfort to a halt. That wasn't working, so I began sticking one of my fingers down my throat to see if that would work. I busted many of the blood vessels around my eyes because my face was straining along with my stomach to win this battle against this unknown intruder that had made its way into my gut.

My wife took me to our family doctor's office. I was running an intermittent fever. My stomach pains had subsided, but I was very sick. I felt very weak. I had to struggle to sit up in one of the chairs in their waiting room. I just wanted to lie down, and I did so on the table inside the examination room where one of the nurses had led us. There, I shut my eyes while we waited for the doctor. After checking me over thoroughly, he told us that I was the sickest patient he had seen in over a year.

His staff ran some blood tests in hopes of determining what was wrong with me. The results showed that my white blood cell count was highly elevated, which meant that I probably had an infection somewhere in my body.

The next step was to do a computerized tomography (CT) scan to determine what was going on inside of me. Their findings showed that I had some abnormality in the lower right quadrant of my abdomen. My doctor originally guessed that he thought I could have meningitis. Now, after reviewing the scans, he thought I probably had appendicitis. He believed there was a distant chance that I had an irritable bowel syndrome, such as Crohn's disease. The latter is an autoimmune disease where the body attacks itself. My doctor said that we could wait to see if I got better, or he could send me to see a surgeon.

"I can't miss any more work. I would like to see someone who can help me get back on my feet as soon as possible," I said in desperation, hoping it would be sooner than later.

It was Good Friday. I was lying on an operating table in the hospital. I was about to go under anesthesia. My surgeon was going to look inside of me laparoscopically to explore my guts to find out why I was so sick. I was hoping it wasn't anything seriously wrong with me.

When I woke up in the recovery room, I was in severe pain. The nurse said I could push the button on a device she placed in my hand whenever I felt pain. I began pushing it non-stop.

"Mr. Seaver, you only need to push it one time. The pain medication is morphine. You can only release the amount of dosage into your system as prescribed by your surgeon," my nurse said, trying to get me to stop pushing.

"Why am I in so much pain? Where are you taking me?" I asked the nurse.

"There is a tornado in the area, so we are moving you into the hallway for your safety," she said, trying to assure me that I was safer there.

I was groggy from the anesthesia. I fell back asleep and woke up in my room that the hospital assigned to me.

I was told that the tornado had lifted into the air as it passed over the hospital without doing any damage.

My doctor was standing in my hospital room, where I was lying in what I thought might be my death bed. My wife was standing on my right side. She held my hand, and I held my breath.

"You have Crohn's disease. I had to remove your appendix along with some of your small intestine and large colon that were all blackened and diseased."

That explains why I was hurting so badly, I thought.

I had a large incision on the right side of my stomach. It was being held together by some staples. I also had a small opening where a tube was allowing any remaining infection to drain out.

Later, I was told that I would probably have to change my diet and lifestyle. I also learned it was likely that I would battle this disease for the rest of my life. In the event of any reoccurrences, more surgeries would be the only cure available. Death would probably be the outcome when someone no longer has any of their healthy colon left.

"God, why is this happening to me? Are you punishing me for all the times I have hurt You and my wife by cheating on both of you with men? For my other sinful ways? I know that I deserve this judgment," I prayed.

My prayers hit the ceiling and bounced right back into my confused heart. I wasn't feeling His presence like when I had prayed in my other times of trouble. Heaven was silent.

My wife stayed close by my side as much as she was able to do while working and taking care of our two sons. At first, she had told me she thought that I wasn't that sick. She thought that I might even be faking my illness (really?). After my surgery, she knew she was wrong. She began praying that God would save her husband once again.

The counselor from my men's support group came and prayed with me in the hospital. Some of the men from the group did too. I was so blessed that they cared enough to come and see me. My heart became tender in a way it hadn't been before. Any gesture of love or concern for me would bring tears to my eyes almost immediately.

I will never forget the last night I was in the hospital. I was praying to God, even though it felt as if He wasn't listening. Suddenly, the atmosphere changed in the room. The presence of God was so thick. I couldn't see Jesus, but I knew He was there. Tears of relief and healing flowed down my cheeks. I began thanking Him for not abandoning me.

The next morning (Sunday), I was released from the hospital. I had been in there for ten days. My wife took me home. It was difficult to walk up the steps to our apartment. My body was still weak from my surgery. My wife took great care of me over the next few weeks. She doctored my wounds and changed my bandages regularly as needed. What a gift of God she was to me.

I must tell you that the Holy Spirit was ministering to me even more than my wife was doing. I could hear His voice in such an amazing way. It wasn't audible, but it was loud and clear. He was healing my heart in ways that I didn't know it needed.

My wife worked at a childcare program that was being run by a large organization. She was great with kids. They welcomed her love and humor that she freely gave to them. This was the same job she had in our hometown before she moved to Louisville. It just so happened that a similar position opened here with this same organization. They chose her to fill it.

One afternoon, my wife came into the apartment with anger painted on her face.

"I hate my job. I want to quit, but I know that I can't," she said.

I had quit my job at the mortgage company after I learned what a disservice was being done to many of our clients. I didn't want to harm anyone financially. I wasn't going to take advantage of someone who needed my help so I could make a living for my family. There had to be another job where I could work and not hurt anyone. After I discovered what was going on at my job, the Holy Spirit told me to quit my job. He asked me to trust Him to provide one that wouldn't compromise my convictions.

My wife's income was all that we were living on, so therefore, she thought that quitting wasn't an option for her.

"Tell her to quit her job," the Holy Spirit said to me.

I obediently told her what He said.

"Quit your job, honey."

"Are you crazy? I can't quit my job. Greg, what will we do for money?" she said with a look of disbelief on her face.

"We will trust God. He said to quit, so that's what you should do."

Reluctantly, my wife did as God suggested. She had two weeks of vacation pay that she was given as she left her unwanted job behind.

She sent out her resume and landed a job with an organization that cared for kids who needed a big brother or big sister in their lives.

She found a job she could love that reached out to love and support many kids who didn't have enough due to their family dynamics and circumstances. She was offered this opportunity a week and a half after she had quit her job. Her new office, where she would be working at, was in a building in downtown Louisville on the sixth floor.

I sent out my resume along with prayers to God that He would only open the door for the job He wanted me to have. It wasn't too long when I got hired by a large bank in Louisville. They offered me a mortgage loan officer position. I was given a three-month salary, but after that period, I would go on straight commission only.

At the end of the three months, the bank offered me a salaried position. I was assigned to a bank branch where I would have an office to meet prospective customers who needed a mortgage. Of all the branches in Louisville (there were many all over the city), guess where mine was? It was in the same building on the first floor, where my wife was now working on the sixth floor.

Can you believe it? I was amazed and knew that only God could pull off something like this.

I recovered fully from my Crohn's surgery over the next few months. I began taking vitamin B-12 injections monthly. It was recommended that I do so because I had some of my small intestine removed. I was told that it is believed that vitamin B-12 is only absorbed into your system by this organ. I am not an expert in this matter. This is what I remember being told by my gastrointestinal specialist.

He also told me that there was a drug that I could take to try to prevent me from having a reoccurrence with Crohn's. I believe he told me that there was a 50/50 chance that it could come back. The decision I was facing was just like flipping a coin.

Like I told you, I believed Jesus had walked into my hospital room the night before I went home. I believed that He had healed me.

"I don't want to take any medicine at this time. If for some reason the Crohn's does recur, then we can discuss medications then," I said to my specialist.

"It's your decision to make, not mine," he said with a look on his face that wasn't as confident as the one on mine.

I smiled and thanked him for seeing me.

After a few months, I decided to opt out of taking a B-12 injection to see what the results would be. I had my doctor send some of my blood off to a lab to be tested. The results showed that my level was good. I haven't taken another vitamin shot to this day.

I was able to resume my normal activities. I was back in the gym lifting weights. I began playing sand volleyball again. My diet didn't change, but food ran through my digestive system quicker than previously because there was less distance for it to travel.

My unwanted homosexual desires came back too. I didn't know if any men would still be attracted to me because I now had a large scar along with a smaller one on my abdomen from my surgery. Just being honest. I had learned to try to be ready for rejection so it might not hurt as bad when it happened.

19

"Greg, how could you do this to me again? I can't do this anymore," my wife said with deep pain in her voice.

"I told you I am not going to leave you for another man like I have in the past," I responded, trying to reassure her.

"I can't keep letting you hurt me like this. I just can't," she said, fighting back the tears that were welling up in her eyes.

I had another boyfriend that I had been seeing, and she had just found out about him. I had left my pager behind while I was away at a volleyball tournament. He had left me a message on it telling me that he was missing me while I was away. She had listened to it and was now confronting me about what she had just learned.

All my wife's hope of her being happy in her marriage to a gay man had drained from her face. It seemed as if she had been backed into the corner of an invisible prison cell where she was being emotionally tormented.

Some time passed after that revelation of her marital bondage when she believed she may have found a means of escape. Had she just heard her cell door unlock with the hope of being set free?

"Greg, I have been seeing someone, and things are getting serious. He's the guy I slept with while you were away visiting your parents years ago," my wife said.

It wasn't easy trying not to appear upset by her news, but I managed to keep my poker face on, pretending to be okay with what I had just heard.

Her happy expression about the possibility of something working out between them turned into one of disbelief because of what she was seeing on my face.

"I can't believe you don't care! Aren't you going fight for me like I have for you all these years?" she asked.

"I want you to be happy. I don't think I can be the man who can make that happen for you," I said with a sadness inside that I hoped she couldn't detect in my voice.

I was about to watch her go after her own happiness without me, like she had watched me pursue mine without her so many times in our past.

"You don't care about my happiness! You see a way out for you to finally be gay, and you are taking it," she said back to me.

I am not going to lie. She was partly right. I still believed that I was gay and would only be completely happy if I was with the right guy. It was unfair for her to be with a man that was never going to be what she needed for him to be.

I had tried to be the guy I thought my wife needed. I always felt like I was never enough. Maybe she must have felt like she wasn't enough either?

There were many times in our marriage when I wasn't sleeping around. We had been through so much in our lives together. We could always talk about almost anything. We were both as open as we could be about how we felt during both our good and bad times together.

We sang together at the top of our lungs in our car on road trips. She never seemed to mind that I was monotone and couldn't sing very well. Her singing skill was far superior to mine. She had a beautiful alto voice. She sounded a lot like Karen Carpenter. It was as if she had music accompanying her when she sang a cappella.

I was envious of her talent. She had competed in several talent shows and won first place in many of them. She was a songwriter too.

She loved God like I did. We laughed together. We cried together. I could depend on her to be there for me like no one else on earth besides God.

Over the course of the next several weeks, I began trying to let go of my wife. I didn't let her know about the deep emotions I was feeling about her. Through quiet tears that I never let her see, I said goodbye to her in my heart.

It was a lot harder than I thought it was going to be. We had grown up together because we were so young when we got married. We had been together for over seventeen years. I told myself that I had to be strong for her. I couldn't let her know that I didn't know how I was going to make it without her.

I turned my heart towards my boyfriend because I believed that was the only choice left to make. I was gay, so I shouldn't be with my wife regardless of how I felt about her. I had sexual desires for her at the beginning of our marriage. Those desires became ambivalent over time. They would wane and then resurface after she would take me back after my affairs. They wouldn't last, though. However, the feelings I had for her were deep down, and they were still there.

My wife and I got divorced. We both went our separate ways to pursue happiness apart from one another. Our family was torn into two halves. My oldest son chose to live with me. My youngest son moved out of town with his mother when she left. My boyfriend moved into my apartment with me shortly thereafter.

From the beginning, he allowed me to control things in our relationship, which helped me to feel safe. We had met each other at a gay bar. He was different than any of the other guys I had met. One of the best words to describe him was "genuine." He was down to earth. His mother had raised him well. Maybe this time, it will work out for me?

He had to drive two hours to his job every morning and two hours back to my place. It was in his hometown, which was south of Louisville. He never complained about it, as far as I can remember.

He tolerated my neurosis that I was rapidly developing. I was paranoid about him cheating on me. Over the years, I had seen some gay guys cheating on their lovers when they weren't looking. There were some couples who had open relationships where either one was free to sleep around. Others were having threesomes together. Besides being aware of these kinds of relationships, my ex-wife and I had cheated on each other. I didn't want any part of another open relationship. My boyfriend lovingly tried to reassure me that he had no intentions of straying, but my heart had difficulty believing him.

I looked my boyfriend in the eyes. It had been a few months after he had moved in with me.

"If this relationship doesn't work for me, then I believe I will be done with this gay stuff. I want to give us every chance to make our relationship work. Let's have Bible studies together. Let's go to church together. Let's keep ourselves away from any sexual temptations," I said while studying his face to see if he understood how serious mine was.

He agreed to do what I wanted in order to make our relationship last. He said that he wanted the same things that I did. Our feelings for each other were mutual. We both believed that we were in love. We both didn't want to lose each other, no matter what might try to stand in our way.

We decided to join the church that we had begun attending together. We didn't dare tell them the truth about us because they wouldn't have let us join. They asked us if we were baptized believers. I said that I had been baptized many years ago. My boyfriend told them that he hadn't been baptized yet but that he wanted to be.

After he got baptized, we joined the church. We didn't share anything about our relationship with anyone there. We weren't asked any questions, fortunately. No one there knew our secret but God Himself.

We bought a big house together. He nor I had ever owned a home before. I was making a lot of money in the mortgage industry. I was driving an expensive car, and so was he. From a financial standpoint, you could say we were living the American dream. I had everything that I thought would make me happy.

One night, I had a conversation with my dad. He had a very loving tone in his voice when he said these words to me.

"Greg, I know you have tried to overcome homosexuality in every way available to you. I know you are pursuing a life that you think is going to make you happy, but son, it's not God's will for you. I don't believe it will work."

"Dad, thanks for loving me. I know you have prayed and prayed for me regarding homosexuality. I appreciate it. This is something I need to do. I am happy. We are going to church together."

God was helping me in my relationship with my boyfriend, which baffled me. If my dad was right that my relationship wasn't God's will, then why was He helping me? What I mean by helping me is that He talked to me about my neurosis. He challenged me about my feelings, how I was acting, how I was treating my boyfriend, and so on. I expected Him to abandon me after my divorce. I was now fully embracing my homosexuality, but God was somehow still in the picture.

20

I am not sure how long I stayed faithful in my relationship with my boyfriend. I believe it was at least two years or longer. My sexual desire for him waned. I grew restless, just like I had in my marriage with my wife. I started to seek out other men for sex. I began going out to sing karaoke at gay bars. This provided opportunities for temptations to occur with guys that I would meet at the bars. This progressed to me seeking out other encounters to hook up in other ways. I started cruising parks, online chatrooms, adult bookstores, and bathhouses to meet guys for anonymous sex.

One night, I was out singing at a gay karaoke bar. I met a guy there. We struck up a conversation about singing. He had lived in Nashville in the past. He was a singer who had pursued his dream of having a career in country music. I was intrigued due to my passion for singing.

After the bar closed, we wound up going to a motel nearby. We made a connection. It resulted in us starting to hang out on a regular basis after that night. We went out singing karaoke at various bars. Some were gay and some were straight clubs. I was not having sex at home, but I was with my side guy. We were having fun. He was encouraging me in my singing. Something that my boyfriend didn't do.

I did not leave my boyfriend for him because of something that happened between this man and myself. I am choosing not to disclose the details of it in this book. Eventually, he and I were able to move past the incident. We reconciled our relationship but in a platonic way. We are still friends to this day.

I had another gay buddy that I went on a trip with to Orlando. We stayed at an all-gay resort for several days. We got separate rooms, but neither of us was alone in our rooms for most of the trip.

We were out riding in our rental car when I looked out the window at a large billboard. It had a question written on it in big, bold letters: ***ARE YOU TIRED?*** Around the border of the sign was the ministry name, Exodus International. I had heard of Exodus. It was a ministry that worked with people who wanted to leave the gay lifestyle. To be honest, I was tired of my promiscuity. I was not getting a lot out of my sexual encounters anymore. My gay relationship with my boyfriend, which had lasted over eight years, was all but over. I was pursuing a life that I thought would have made me happy, but I was anything but happy.

I deboarded the airplane that had brought us back from Florida. I got into my car and drove home. I had almost gotten to my house when God spoke these words to me.

"Greg, how many guys do you need to sleep with before you realize this gay life is not going to work for you? You have a guy at home who let you control him and everything in your lives together. He even went to church with you. Everything that you have tried or are currently trying hasn't made you happy."

"No, I am not happy. God, You know that I have tried in the past to change unsuccessfully. I will try one more time, but You must help me."

By this time, I was in tears. The Holy Spirit began surging inside of me as I prayed. The best way to describe what I experienced was like a powerful current of energy. This sensation started traveling from my feet and continued all the way up my legs and into my chest. I had never experienced Him in this way before that day.

The very next day, I got online and searched for Exodus International. It just so happened that they were hosting their international conference not too far from where I was living in Indiana. I clicked on the link to view the itinerary for the conference. It informed me about which speakers would be presenting at their main sessions, along with various topics that were going to be covered in workshops as well.

The Holy Spirit spoke to me again.

"If you are serious about getting help, then you will sign up for the entire week of meetings."

So, I did just what I was encouraged to do by God. I signed up for the whole conference.

I was excited and hopeful as I drove northbound to the college campus that was hosting the Exodus conference. I got checked in and found my assigned room, which was in one of their dormitories. Most of the students weren't on campus because it was summertime. I dropped off my suitcase and headed to the first session.

I was quite shocked at how many people were in attendance. There were close to one thousand men and women in the room from all over the United States and some outside of our country. A worship band was on stage, leading everyone in praise and worship of Jesus. I began to cry because I had this realization that I wasn't the only one. There were hundreds of people there who were worshipping God while struggling with desires that were in conflict with the Bible at the same time that I was.

As I walked to where lunch was being served, I began to look at the faces of the people that I was passing by on the sidewalk. I do not know exactly how to describe it except that I was beholding my own brokenness on many of their faces. It was daunting, to say the least.

I cried during every session. Most of them included someone sharing their testimony. One of the testimonies that I heard overwhelmed me. A lady who had been an atheist found God just in time before she killed herself. Her marriage was falling apart, and her son had just announced that he was gay. She boarded a train that was destined to arrive in the city where her son was living. She was going there to see him one last time before she ended her life. But God miraculously intervened by saving her soul. She began to pray for her husband and her son. God answered her prayers by saving her husband along with her marriage.

In the next night's session, the woman's son gave his testimony. The crazy thing is that I knew her son. I had met him through one of my boyfriends in the past. He had moved to Atlanta. He dropped out of college and became a drug dealer. His mother prayed to God to please do whatever it took to save her son.

Her answer came in an unexpected way. Several FBI agents knocked on his door. They confiscated a very large quantity of drugs. They arrested him. He was sentenced to six years in prison. While he was locked up, he found God. He served three years of his sentence before he was released early because of God's intervention. He applied to attend a Christian college. He enclosed letters of recommendation from the warden and another prison official. He was surprised that he was accepted. He started attending once he was released. When he walked out of that prison, his gay lifestyle stayed behind. I talked with him briefly after the meeting. He was as surprised to see me there as I was to see him.

One day, at lunchtime, I usually sat with some of the guys, but I found myself sitting with some ladies instead. One of the ladies shared her testimony. It was very powerful because not only did she leave the lifestyle, but her partner of twenty-one years also left the lifestyle. I found out that this woman only lived about ten minutes from where I lived. We exchanged numbers so we could meet up once we got back home.

Many of us had roommates during the conference. This helped to keep our enrollment costs down to a minimum. One night, in my room, I was sharing with my roommate. He told me that he had been sexually abused by a close family member. I began feeling waves of supernatural compassion flowing out of me toward him. These were the same kind that flowed out of me when I had been preaching while my boyfriend at the time was in the congregation (I told you about this earlier in the book). I was blown away that I was experiencing this from the Holy Spirit again.

"Wow, God really loves you!" I said with a gentle but amazed tone.

"Why would you say that?" he responded with a look of disbelief.

"I am feeling these powerful love waves coming out of me. They are flowing towards you. I wish you could feel what I am feeling."

"I wish I could feel it too because I don't believe it."

I tried to reassure him that I was telling him the truth, but I don't think I succeeded. He was a very kind, soft-spoken man. He was confused about a lot of things where God was concerned. He was also confused about his sexuality too.

The conference ended. Many of us hugged each other as we said our goodbyes. I did not know that I could cry as much as I did that week. I was emotionally drained as a result. I did not act out sexually with anyone during my time at the conference. I was hit on by one of the guys, but I resisted his advances. I will admit that there were several good-looking guys that I saw there. I was not there to cruise but to pursue getting the help that I needed.

When I got back home, I had an immediate conversation with my boyfriend.

"I am leaving the gay lifestyle. You and I need to start sleeping in separate bedrooms."

"We aren't having sex together, so I don't see why it's an issue?"

"I just don't feel right about us sleeping in the same bed anymore. I don't believe it's something we should do."

I was adamant. He could see that I wasn't about to change my mind. Our house had three other bedrooms that were vacant. He reluctantly chose to sleep in one of them as I had demanded.

21

I was sitting at a coffee shop. Across from me sat the lady I had met at the Exodus conference. Her name is Cindy. We had only been talking for a few minutes, but I could quickly tell something was unique about this woman that I hadn't detected at the conference. She was very easy to talk to about some things that I wouldn't bother sharing with most people. Because she had walked down a similar path that I was walking, I knew she had a very good idea about what I was going through. I could tell that God had helped her on her journey. I was excited to share with her what I had been learning about myself and God. How rare must it be to find someone who not only understands you but makes you feel like you can tell them anything? I say that because she wasn't holding a gavel of judgment in one hand while she held her coffee in the other.

We started hanging out regularly after that first meeting. She invited me to go with her to a monthly support group that she attended. This group was for friends and family members who had loved ones who identified as gay. She went on a regular basis because she wanted to support these people who were concerned by what they believed the Bible had to say about homosexuality. They feared that the people they loved were in danger of eternal destruction.

I remember my first night at the group. I went into the meeting with a chip on my shoulder. As I told you, I had read many books about how someone becomes gay. The authors believed that parents play a vital role in how a child's identity develops. Therefore, my intentions, in the beginning, were to point out how they were partly at fault for their kids being gay. My anger was quickly diffused. I saw pain and anguish on their faces. Many cried as they shared what they were going through. They talked about how they had raised their children to believe in God. They said that many of their loved ones had professed to believe in Jesus as their Savior, but somewhere along the way, some had walked away from their faith. Others believed that God was okay with their gay lifestyles because they believed they were born that way. My heart started breaking for them because most of theirs was already broken. I would grow to love all of them during the times we shared together.

Because I had read that passive fathers were a factor in boys becoming homosexual, I wrote a letter to my father trying to repair our relationship. The letter didn't produce the response from my father that I had hoped. Eventually, I quit trying because I believed that it would never happen.

After giving up hope, God stepped in and did what only He can do.

I boarded a plane that was headed to Dallas, Texas. My dad was waiting there at the airport to pick me up and take me home with him. I was going there to spend the week with him and my stepmom.

When I saw him standing outside of the terminal, I felt like I was a little boy again. But this time, my feelings were loving towards him, unlike most of mine in the past. I hugged him, and then we walked to his truck to leave.

One night, we were out on his patio drinking some wine. He had built a fire that was blazing in his outdoor fireplace. My stepmom was sitting out there with us.

"Dad, do you remember the day I helped you put up a chain-linked fence around our backyard?"

"Yes, I do."

"Well, later that night, Mom told me that you were very proud of how hard I worked mixing and wheelbarrowing loads of cement to you. I didn't need to hear those words from my mother. I needed to hear them directly from you," I said with a conviction that must have come from the wine.

He put his hand over his face as tears began to flow from his eyes.

"Greg, I did the best that I knew how on raising you when you were growing up."

My stepmother jumped up and started sweeping off the patio because she didn't know what else to do in that awkward moment. Then, she excused herself by saying she thought we needed to be alone.

My heart welled up with compassion for him. I had only seen him cry a few times. One of those was after he and I had visited with his father, who was on his deathbed. He had taken me with him to pray with his dad. After I prayed, we went outside to leave. He broke down crying before we got in his car. He knew it wouldn't be long before he would lose him. I tried to comfort him at that moment by putting my arm around him while he cried.

I sat down beside my dad and put my arm around him. I began asking him questions about his relationship with my mom. I also asked him about his relationship with his father. He told me that his dad never told him he loved him. I found out that my grandfather refused to let the doctor cut off my dad's leg when he developed a rare bone disease when he was a little boy. That seemed to be the only redeeming thing that I could say about a man I never knew. I had only seen him a few times in my life before he died.

So, you see, my dad didn't know how to be the dad that I needed him to be because his dad was never someone that he needed him to be either.

We bonded that night in a way that neither one of us expected, but I believe we both needed. We had both been robbed of relationships with each other and my grandfather. It was too late for one of those relationships, but it wasn't too late for ours.

Cindy and her parents started another friends and family group at a church up north closer to where her parents lived. Her mother kept meeting other moms who were devastated about learning the news that one of their children was attracted to the same gender. She wanted these women to have a safe place to share their hearts about this dilemma. Louisville would be too far of a distance for them to travel. They needed somewhere closer to the area where they lived at the time. I went to these meetings with Cindy too. I wanted to help in any way that I could.

Cindy and I also started a support group for men and women who had unwanted same-sex attraction. This approach would differ from the others I attended in the past. Those had been strictly for men except for the very first group. It was the one where it was with a pastor, a lady and myself. Our theory was if men and women share their similar struggles together, then it could help facilitate the healing of their distorted beliefs about the opposite sex they may have had.

We met with these strugglers on a weekly basis in the building where Cindy and I worshipped on Sundays. Our leadership allowed us to meet there. Everyone seemed to be growing close to one another as we endeavored to pursue wholeness in the Lord. Occasionally, some of us would hang out together at a restaurant for dinner and fellowship.

We met with some others by themselves. Many of these were teenagers who still lived with their parents. Most, but not all, were only meeting with us because they were forced to do so. Some were pastors' kids. Others were simply ones who had been raised in a Christian home. Some of the kids seemed to be open and honest about how they were feeling and what they believed. Others were not.

Cindy and I were spending lots of our time in ministry together. We talked on the phone on the days we weren't together in person. We became best friends. I loved hanging out with her. We were very busy in weekly and monthly groups. We were asked to come and give our testimonies at different churches as well. We attended more of the annual Exodus conferences over the next few years.

I decided to quit my job at the bank where I was working. I became upset because I found out one of my bosses was lying to me about some things. Another boss was trying to get me to do something that I believed was ineffective in acquiring more mortgage business.

Please don't think that I was brave or even stupid. I had been on an interview for another job shortly before I made the announcement. I thought that I was surely going to get the position.

My boss told his boss that I was quitting. She found me standing by my desk. I had just finished putting all my personal items in a box. She asked me if I would accompany her somewhere privately to discuss why I was quitting. I agreed to do so because I cared about this woman. She had been very supportive to me in the past. She was the first person at work that I came out to after my divorce. I was drunk at one of her work parties when I confessed to her that the guy who was there with me was more than just a friend. She took the news in stride. She knew him because I had helped him get a job there. After learning this news, she agreed to allow us to continue working in the same office together. She didn't understand why we had to be together all the time, but she tolerated it for me. I had developed a neurosis where I felt I needed to be with him to feel safe.

We were sitting down when I told her that I believed that she had lied to me about some things. She didn't confirm or deny my allegations. Instead, she asked me to think things over carefully and call her the next day to let her know if I had changed my mind.

I prayed and asked God if I was making the right decision. Afterward, I had peace, so I believed I was in His will. Besides, I was hoping that He would eventually take me out of secular work altogether and move me into full-time ministry. That was my dream for the future that I was holding onto at that moment.

He must know that I am going to get the other job where I had interviewed, I thought to myself.

The next morning, I picked up my phone and called my boss out of my respect for her. She answered. I took a deep breath.

"Hi, it's Greg. I am calling to tell you that I am quitting. I prayed about it. I believe that I am supposed to quit."

"I appreciate you letting me know like I had asked. I hope you know what you are doing because I think it's a mistake. I wish you good luck in whatever you pursue in the future."

As soon as I hung up with her, I felt a warm, unseen blanket covering me. I had only felt this kind of sensation one other time. It was when I stayed with my friend (the one I lost my virginity with) and her family years earlier. Her mom was a Christian. I had been reading a book on how Satan was alive and well on the planet earth. I had lots of questions about God that came up as I was reading this book. I had also bought a Bible and was reading it too. She and I had conversations throughout the course of my stay with them. I asked her some of my questions. She confided in me about some things she was going through in her marriage.

One night, after we had talked, I went to their study and laid down to go to sleep. She had made some space in this room so I could sleep on a pallet there instead of being in her daughter's room. As I was lying there, I felt as if someone else had entered the room. I sensed it was Satan in there with me, but I couldn't see him. I became terrified! I desperately whispered a prayer to God to please rescue me. Suddenly, a warm blanket was covering me. I felt safe and became unafraid. I drifted off to sleep.

Now, I was lying in my bed with the same unseen warm blanket covering me. This time, I believed God was telling me that I was financially safe and in His will. I tried to relax as I fought off thoughts of doubt about what I had just done. I don't think I had lost my mind. However, I believe Cindy, along with almost everyone else, may have thought I had when I told them that I had quit the job that had paid me very well over the years.

The next morning, I was lying in bed when the Holy Spirit spoke to me.

"Get up! You have this time off from work, and you need to

utilize it to the best of your ability."

I was shaken by what He had just said to me. I was obedient and got up.

I began to read several books (usually one chapter in each one) every day, including the Bible. One of the books I read was about having a purpose-driven life. I will never forget about reading the chapter that talked about how Abraham and Moses were friends with God. I was sitting on a stool in my kitchen. The Holy Spirit grabbed my heart. It was as if He had His hand wrapped around it. The sensation I was experiencing was almost unbearable. I got up and wobbled into my bedroom. I was crying uncontrollably. I fell onto my knees and placed my face to the floor as I wailed. He didn't let go of my heart until He was sure that I *knew* He was *my* friend too. There's a statement that Jesus made that is recorded in the Bible. No greater love is there than a man laying down his own life for his friends.

I made my way back into the kitchen. I was standing in there singing to Him. When I finished the song, He spoke these words to me.

"Greg, I want you to be all about Me, because I am all about you."

I cried again after hearing Him speak those words to my heart.

"I want to believe You," I whispered back to Him.

22

I began writing songs.

One song I wrote was influenced by someone who had been sexually abused by some members of her family. I met her through Cindy. She had asked me to help her minister to this woman. She was stuck on her journey to wholeness. She couldn't get past the shame and hurt she had experienced. She seemed to blame herself instead of the ones who had injured her so deeply. Some of my pain had been inflicted by someone in my family. Mine were verbal wounds, though. "Don't Know Why" is the name of the song.

I wrote another song after watching a movie about a gay man trying to find love. He found someone, but the guy was extremely hot and cold toward him for various reasons. The lyrics poured out of me onto the page in a matter of about ten minutes. Five minutes after the words were written, I had a melody. The song "Someone to Love" may be about what most of us long for in this world.

Another song that I wrote was about *all things* being *possible* to those who believe. I was so excited about the song that I couldn't wait to call and share it with Cindy. She liked the song and the words.

One morning, I was sitting in my kitchen with my Bible opened.

"God, please give me a song right out of Your Word."

I found my way, or I was led to John 14, where Jesus says, "If you ask Me anything in My name, I will do it" (John 14:14, NASB). The song "In My Name" was born.

Many other songs were birthed during this time. They were written when I was stirred up emotionally or when I was being overwhelmed by the compassion and love of God. I wrote each lyric with prayer. After writing the words, I would ask God for a melody. He gave me one every time I asked Him.

Do you remember what I told you earlier about my singing? How awful it was?

A few years earlier, I had bought a karaoke system. I practiced and practiced singing. I was determined to get my ability to at least a place where people could tolerate my voice without laughing or talking about me behind their backs. I practiced so much that my vocal cords would hurt for several days afterward. Once the pain subsided, I would turn the machine on and start singing again. I had this unquenchable desire to sing.

When I believed that I had gotten to the place where I could somewhat carry a tune, I ventured out to some places that had karaoke.

One night, I met a guy who told me that he was taking vocal lessons. His teacher was attempting to get him to try and write his own songs. My ears perked up because I thought maybe his vocal coach could help me sing better. He gave me her contact information. I called her in hopes that she would agree to work with me. She accepted, and I was elated. I was hoping that she might be a miracle worker.

I was standing next to her while she sat on a bench in front of her piano. The room seemed to get brighter each time she smiled as she spoke to me about singing. There was an undeniable warmth in her voice that made me feel at home and safe to be in her presence. Her eyes were like pools of compassion when she looked at me. I had never met anyone like her before. She began leading me through some breathing exercises. Then, she led me through some vocal warmups. She asked me what song I wanted to sing for her. I played one for her on my phone that I knew. Immediately, she started trying to find the chords she was hearing. She pressed her fingers on the piano keys, searching for the tempo and melody. She had an amazing gift and could play by ear. She mastered the song in no time at all. She played it on her keyboard while I accompanied her with my voice.

"Honey, you have a beautiful voice," she said with big eyes.

"Thank you," I said back to her while being in shock about what she had just said.

I didn't believe her even though she had said it with conviction.

"You should be singing with a band. Your voice would be perfect to lead one."

"That would be awesome! I just don't know of any bands I could sing with," I said back to her before I realized that she was causing me to almost believe her.

"Have you ever thought about writing a song?"

"I can't even play an instrument, so how could I write a song?"

"Just try writing something about your life. See where that takes you."

Later that night, I sat down and started to write. I told you I had written poetry in the past. Somehow, I knew that I needed to meter out the syllables in each line. I prayerfully began writing lines about how I hoped to find what I needed in someone. "Right Out of the Blue" was the name that I gave to the song that I wrote.

At our next session, I told her that I had written a song. She looked surprised and asked me to share it with her. I showed her the lyrics and began trying to sing the melody that I was feeling. I got excited as she began to play and sing back to me what she was hearing.

My vocal teacher and I began to become friends over the next several weeks. She shared her heart with me about things in her life. She was a believer and was a music minister in her church. I shared with her that I was a believer too. I told her that I was gay and in a relationship with a man. I told her that I was conflicted about where I was in my life because of my faith.

"My ex-husband is gay and has AIDS. One of my sons is gay too," she said with tears in her eyes.

She went on to tell me how hard it was for her to deal with her *son when she first learned the news that he was gay. Her faith caused a lot of conflict for her. They were asked to leave one of the churches they attended because of him. He unsuccessfully attempted to commit suicide. She went through emotional turmoil as she fought to save his life from destruction. Most people in their church were rejecting him. She wasn't going to be another person to do the same thing. She prayed for him. She loved him and walked with him through his pain of feeling unwanted.*

I sat down at a picnic table in a park in Louisville. I thought about what this woman had shared with me about her life and her son. I thought about what I had gone through in my life for being gay. At that moment, I believe God let me feel things I hadn't felt or blocked out. I also tried to empathize with what others may have felt too. The song "Unwanted" came pouring out of me. In the chorus, I wrote that I heard You (Jesus) were rejected too. I believe He had felt very similar feelings about being unwanted when the crowd was crying out that Pilate should have Him crucified! Before that had happened, Judas, one of his disciples, betrayed Him with a kiss in the garden of Gethsemane. Finally, when He was hanging on the cross, He cried out, "My God, My God, why have You forsaken Me?" (Matthew 27:46, NASB).

This was how my songwriting had begun. If I had this ability from birth, it had been hidden from me. It may have been something that God developed in me by faith as I put my pen to the page. When I opened up my mouth to try and sing what my heart was feeling, notes began to flow out of me.

23

Things seemed to be really going great. Ministry was at the forefront of my life. I was content being single. I believed that I didn't need to be in a loving relationship with someone because I had God to fill that void.

I told you about the karaoke buddy that I had an affair with that ended with us just being friends. He asked me if I wanted to go to Mexico with him. He had some free airline tickets. He also worked for a hotel chain, so he was able to get a room at a discounted employee rate. He knew I couldn't afford it, so the trip was going to be covered by him. The reason was because I wasn't working anywhere because I had quit my job. I loved Mexico. I had been there a few times already. It was one of my favorite places in the world. I jumped at his offer to go with him.

We stayed at an all-inclusive resort. I had way too much to drink one night. Somehow, we wound up going to a gay nightclub in the area. We met someone, and he came back to our hotel with us. I was still intoxicated. I must have left all my resistance to having sex with a man back in the United States.

"You are out of the country. No one will know what you did," I told myself.

I believed my buddy wouldn't tell anyone what was about to happen.

These thoughts flashed quickly through my mind. I was either lying to myself, or I had a devil whispering them to me. I am not sure which one or both might have been happening inside my head that night.

I fell homosexually again.

My guilt began to eat me for breakfast the next morning.

I drank too much the rest of the time I was in Mexico. I was trying to drown my emotions. I was upset because I had once again slept with another man. I was dejected. Here, I was supposed to be a leader in ex-gay ministry, but I had fallen prey to my drunken temptations.

"What a joke you are! Are you trying to deceive yourself or just everyone else that you aren't gay anymore?" I said to myself with as much disdain as I could muster.

When I got back, I didn't confess what I had done to Cindy or anyone else for that matter.

I had been hanging out a lot with one of the guys from our support group. He was depressed because he was struggling to rebuild his life. He had distanced himself from his old gay friends. He wasn't being successful in connecting with anyone at his church. He was lonely. He cried often about what he was experiencing as he tried to do what he believed God was asking him to do. I felt empathy for him, so I tried to spend as much time as I could to help him cope with his loneliness.

This man was glad that I called to tell him that I was back in town. He told me that he had missed me while I was away.

The next night, I went over to his place after one of my volleyball league matches was over. He had come to watch me play. His place wasn't too far from where I had played my match.

We were sitting on his couch, talking about my trip to Mexico. It was a small sofa, so we were sitting very close to each other. He reached down and started rubbing on my stomach. He had never done anything like this before. I didn't stop him from rubbing on me. Maybe it was because my guilty thoughts were dwelling on my fall abroad. I wanted to tell him what had happened to me while I was away. We had become emotionally codependent. Something I had been in most of my relationships, including my relationship with my ex-wife.

I became aroused because of how he was rubbing on me. I jumped up and made my way quickly to his front door. He grabbed my arm and stopped me before I was able to escape. I told him that I should leave.

"Please don't leave. I am sorry for whatever I did wrong."

I turned around and looked him in the eyes. He had a look of such deep pain in them.

"I really should go. Things are getting out of hand here."

I didn't run, but I wish that I had because the next thing that I knew, we locked lips. My resolve had left, but I was still in his house. We headed upstairs and fell into his bed.

I want to interject that I had never had a sexual attraction to him before that night. My motives were pure. I was simply trying to help him. I wound up giving in to his advances at a very vulnerable time after a fall. The Bible says that *pride* goes before destruction and a *haughty* spirit before stumbling in Proverbs 16:18. I thought I was safe to be alone with him. I thought that I wouldn't be tempted to have sex with him because I wasn't attracted to him physically.

He and I had a few more encounters over the next few weeks. We registered to attend an upcoming Exodus conference. We were going to stay in the same room together. I told myself that I had apparently lost my mind. I decided I had to do something drastic to end what was happening. I wasn't about to go to a conference for a week with someone that I could possibly be falling with the whole time I was there. That would defeat every purpose for going.

I attempted to commit ministry suicide. I was disgusted with myself. I wanted to no longer be in ministry of any kind, especially ex-gay ministry. I went and confessed what I had done to the leader of our ministry. She was very loving. I expected judgment. I thought that she would toss me out of the ministry and slam the proverbial door in my face. But she didn't, even though I wanted her to. She told me that I needed to tell Cindy. That was one of the hardest things that I had to do. She was the last person I wanted to hurt or let down at the time.

Surprisingly, she wasn't that surprised when I told her what had happened. She confessed that many people (including her) saw how he and I had grown very close. She resisted confronting me about it. Now, she was regretting not doing so.

The leader and Cindy chose to walk beside me in hopes of seeing me restored to sexual sobriety and wholeness. I stepped down from leadership. They, along with another male leader, also attempted to walk alongside the man I had fallen with to see him restored. They recommended that we stay away from being alone together. He wasn't happy about their suggestions. He was angry and told them that he wanted me to help him instead of some of the other leaders in the ministry.

I stayed away from him. We had fallen into a trap that I believe was orchestrated by the enemy of our souls. It wasn't my job to save him, or anyone else for that matter. I couldn't save myself. Why would I think God would need my help in the first place? I guess it was because of the arrogance I unknowingly had. This man was hurt by me. Yes, he was the one who made the first advances. However, I was in leadership. I was the one who should have known better about setting up healthy boundaries for both of us. Unfortunately, he decided to reject the help from the leaders totally. He left the support group and ministry.

I believe it was about two years later when one of the leaders from the church where we were having our meetings called me. He began to ask questions about what had happened between me and this man. I confessed the truth. I told him about what the leaders had chosen to do for both of us. He said that we needed to all meet as soon as possible.

Our leader, Cindy and I were all sitting in a counseling office at the church. The man who had called me was sitting across from us, along with a lady who was in leadership too. I had grown fond of them both over the years. The man had led some men in an ex-gay support group in the past that I had attended. The woman headed up an overcomers program for their members who were struggling with various kinds of addictions. They weren't in authority over us per se, but our ministry support group met weekly in one of the rooms in their church building. Therefore, they had a say in this matter for sure.

They asked me to explain my side of the story about falling sexually with one of our group members. Apparently, he had told someone in their church what had happened to him. The story had found its way to the lead pastor. My confession included my guilt, along with trying to take responsibility for my actions. Cindy and our leader shared how they had worked to ensure that I was restored while I had stepped down from leadership during that time.

Afterward, they asked us what the group rules were. We went over those with them. Their eyebrows raised in what appeared to be expressions of shock. Did they think we had been careless with our group formation? The reason I am wondering is because they kept looking at each other and shaking their heads while we were explaining our group dynamics to them.

"This is something that happened over two years ago. We dealt with it. Nothing like this has occurred since then," our leader said to them, trying to defend our position.

"There is such a stigma on this issue of homosexuality. Greg, I wish you would have come to us when this happened. We would have helped you," the woman said with tears in her eyes.

"I told my leaders. They walked alongside me as I was being restored."

"You should have told us," she said as she moved her eyes away from looking into mine. She shook her head again while she looked down at the floor.

"You need more stringent guidelines. Your group members shouldn't be contacting one another outside of the group," the man said to us.

"We believe that many of our group members feel isolated and alone. We also know that they could easily meet in secret without our knowledge. We are trying to help them begin new lives. Many are leaving behind gay friends and gay meeting places," Cindy responded back to him, trying to explain our position.

"Most of the Exodus groups have guidelines in place to keep someone from falling with another participant," he restated because he hadn't been swayed over to our beliefs.

I wondered to myself if we would be having this meeting if two people from their singles group had slept with each other. I don't think so, but like she said, there's such a "stigma" with this topic.

Other things were discussed as the meeting wound down. The conclusion that manifested was obvious. They were interrogating us to decide if we would be thrown out of their church. Cindy and I wouldn't be barred from attending worship services there but from conducting any more of our ministry at their church. She and I also met privately with people who identified as gay but were wanting to change. We did that regularly in one of their meeting rooms.

A change of venue was looming. An unseen hand didn't write a message on the office wall to tell us that we had been weighed and found wanting, but there was one on their faces.

"You won't get a pink slip in the mail. We will get back to you in person with our decision," the man said with a tone that tried to assure us that he wasn't lying.

Not too much time had transpired from when we had the meeting that I got a call from Cindy asking me to meet with her and one of our leaders.

I met them at a local fast-food restaurant. We sat outside at one of their tables on the patio.

It was easy to tell that Cindy was furious about something. She was holding a letter in her hand.

"They lied about not sending us a pink slip!" Cindy said.

"Are you serious? That's what the letter says? Are they kicking us out of their church?" I asked.

"Yes, they are!" she said back to me with an ache in her voice that she tried to cover with an angry tone.

She couldn't hide it from me. I saw it on her disillusioned face. I had never seen her this upset.

"I can't believe they are doing this!" the other leader said with a dismayed look on his face.

I began having an inner dialogue with myself while they continued to discuss our devastating news.

I am done! I tried to do the right thing when I fell. I confessed to those who were in authority over me. This is what happens when you come clean?

I was on this rant when God interrupted my thoughts.

"You have seen how man does ministry. I am going to show you how I do ministry," the Holy Spirit said in a gentle tone.

Something shifted inside of me when I heard Him say those words to me. It was encouraging, but I was still upset. I was mostly angered because what I had done had affected the rest of the group. They had stood beside me, and now they were paying the price for their grace. Our *unwanted* ministry was going to have to find another place to meet.

24

After not working for almost two years, my retirement savings had dwindled down to almost nothing. I needed to find another job. I found one with a temp agency that provided employees to work at a company that handled flexible spending accounts for various employers. It didn't pay nearly as much as I had made in the past. Over the next several weeks, I saw many of the temporary employees being let go. But for some reason, they didn't fire me. This place was very structured. All your time (breaks, lunches, clocking in, answering inbound phone calls) was constantly being monitored. I didn't like this kind of structure. I had flexibility in my past job as a mortgage loan officer. I hadn't been micro-managed. It suited my personality much more than this current job. I endured it, though, because I felt that I didn't have a choice.

I was leading a singles Bible study group on a weekly basis. These people were praying with me to find a job that would meet my financial needs much better than the temp job where I was working. Cindy attended this group also.

One day, one of the guys in the group called me.

"It just hit me. Maybe you might want to consider working for me? I don't know why I didn't think of this sooner."

He was a district manager for a large company that provided automotive services and repairs.

"Why don't we meet? I can tell you more about what we do. I will also show you the pay structure and what your potential earnings would be with us."

"I really appreciate this offer to meet. I am eager to meet with you as soon as possible," I responded.

Just before we met, I was working at my temp job when one of their managers stopped by my cubicle. He asked me to stop what I was doing and follow him to his office. I thought that I was going to be fired. I took a deep breath as I sat down with him. He told me that I had done a good job for them since I had been there. Then, he offered me a full-time job with his company. The hourly wage that he offered me was two dollars above the amount I was currently making there. His offer included some great benefits and vacation pay.

My buddy from the singles group and I met. He went over their pay structure. He was offering me three dollars more per hour than the flexible spending account company had offered me, plus some sales commissions and good benefits. I accepted his offer.

My first day of work arrived. I was excited to start my new job, but my excitement left my heart as soon as I walked into the store where I had been assigned to work. Immediately, I became overwhelmed with anxiety when I saw all the tires, batteries, wiper blades, and other automotive parts. I had stepped onto foreign soil. I was clueless about where I was standing. I wanted to turn around and walk out of this awkward place of uneasiness that I was experiencing. The other thing that challenged me was the kind of guys that I saw working there. Many of them were rugged, masculine guys. They were comfortable getting dirty and greasy as they worked on cars. Something that I felt I wasn't.

I walked outside behind the store on my lunch break. I pulled out my cell phone and called Cindy. I was pacing back and forth as I told her how I was feeling. While I was talking to her, a revelation hit me. God opened this door of opportunity, so He must know that I can handle this job. Some of my anxiety left me at that moment.

Actually, God had set me up, to be honest. The guy who had hired me has the same first name as my dad. Do you remember the garage scene with my dad that I told you about earlier in the book? I had been invited back into a garage. I was feeling as intimidated as I had been years ago when I was standing looking over my dad's toolbox. Nothing had changed inside of me all these years later.

What did change was the guys in the shop didn't call me a sissy. At least, not to my face. I began to see these kinds of men in a different way. I wasn't hired to work on cars with them, but they relied on me to convince our customers about the maintenance and repairs that they recommended. They were paid based on what kind of work they did and also how long it took for them to complete these repairs and/or services.

After a little over a year working there, I was promoted from a salesman to become our new service manager. This position would entail me overseeing the technicians in the shop along with taking the lead on selling all our services and their recommended repairs to our customers. This would consist of new tires, brakes, fluid exchanges, along with other services. I became successful in this new role. Our lead technician told me that was because people trusted what I told them.

One day, a recruiter came walking into our store. They were looking for employees who would be interested in working in a new venture. They would be providing the same kinds of automotive services, but the shop would be housed in a large retail store. They were opening twelve pilot stores in our local area. Upon it becoming a success, they would open stores across the country. This career opportunity could provide me with the potential to move into becoming a trainer for them. A job that I would prefer over my current position.

I was offered almost two dollars more per hour than I was currently making. I took the offer because of the potential to move up into a more desirable position in the future. I was going to start out being a sales manager for them.

On the first day of training, I was standing outside with some other new employees. The store manager, whom I had been assigned to work with, was standing beside a car. The hood was up. She began explaining what she wanted each of us to learn.

"Why am I being trained to work on cars? I am a sales manager, not a technician," I said in hopes that maybe she didn't know what my position was with her company.

"I know what you were hired to do. I want you to be comfortable with the kind of work we do on cars."

I was not a happy camper. I wanted no part of being underneath the hood of a car. One half of me reluctantly followed her instructions, while the other half thought about leaving.

Later, I called up my old boss to see if I could come back. I explained that I wasn't happy with my new job. This wasn't the same guy who had hired me. He had left and went to work for another company. This guy had looked me in the eye when I quit. He said that he thought I was making a big mistake by leaving. Now, I was eating crow.

"I am afraid I don't have any positions available right now. I hope things work out for you where you are at."

I thanked him for talking with me. I could see that door had been shut in my face with no hopes of it ever opening again.

I had been set up again by God. Not only was I going to sell automotive services, but I was going to be forced into assisting in providing them as well. I was angry. I was extremely intimidated and uncomfortable.

Remember when I told you that my parents sent me to counseling? The first thing my counselor had me to do was take a personality test. The test compiled scores from a range of one up to ten in professions that I would be best suited to. I scored an average of eight in the field of artistic expression. I was somewhat surprised by that number. I would have guessed it to be lower for some reason. I scored a ten in psychology. I was happy about that revelation. But let me tell you, I was extremely surprised that I scored a ten in auto mechanics. I shook my head and laughed. I thought that it must be a fluke because I didn't have an ounce of desire in that field. In fact, I was repulsed by the thought of it.

I don't think that God was laughing, but He was determined to get me to face my intimidations and fears. He succeeded because I forced myself to work on cars when they needed my help. I grew close to my boss, along with other employees. We began hanging out on Sunday evenings at a local pizza restaurant. They had karaoke. I loved to sing so I went almost every weekend with my new friends. We were all bonding in a special way as we worked together and hung out, eating, drinking, and singing together.

I was surprised to find out that our company decided to end its relationship with the retail company. They had tried unsuccessfully to make the venture profitable. Even though I had become more comfortable working on cars, I didn't want to do it for the rest of my working career. I would be forced to work on cars all the time at the other shops this company owned. These were quick service places that specialized in oil changes.

I applied at the retail store for a management position once I had learned how much their managers made. I met their store manager along with many of their other managers. This position would require me to manage the shop they were going to reopen along with the inside automotive parts department.

I sat down with the store manager for an interview. I was shocked that the first words out of his mouth weren't questions he wanted to know about me.

"What's it going to take for you to come and work for us? We have watched you over the past several months. We are impressed with you, and we want you to work for us."

Another manager who was in the room with us nodded in agreement to what was being said by his boss.

"I have heard others talk about what the salary is for this position. If what I heard is true, then I would accept your offer," I said back, hoping that what I had been told was true.

"That is the starting salary, but I am going to try and get you more," he responded back as he smiled at me.

We stood up and shook hands. Now, I was smiling back at him.

He told me that he would get back to me with an offer as soon as possible. My current employer wasn't happy that I wasn't going to stay working for them.

I got the offer. My new boss had kept his word because my starting salary was ten percent higher. He believed it was justified because of my prior experience in the automotive industry.

I became overwhelmed once again. I had fourteen employees whom I was going to oversee. I had to be certified in all the services that we offered. I was unsure of myself, but somehow, I passed my certifications. I also had to learn all the inside operations of our retail store. There was much to learn.

I was blessed to have an experienced service manager who assisted me in running the shop. I had a department manager who was experienced enough to run the inside part of the business with my leadership. I had to trust God to help me with a position that I felt very underqualified to be in at the time. He helped me do what I felt was almost impossible for me.

After three years of enduring a job that was by far the most challenging that I had ever been in before, I was allowed to step down from my position. I stayed employed in the automotive department, but I would now be in the lowest position instead of the highest. I was transferred to another store that wasn't too far away from my current store. It was very humbling, to say the least. I was fortunate in that I was going to be capped out in my hourly pay. This was a financial blessing, even though I would be taking a substantial decrease in my monthly income.

25

As I told you, my boyfriend and I were sleeping in separate bedrooms. One morning, he walked into my bedroom. I was still in my bed, but I was awake. I sat up and looked at him to see what he wanted. He had a nervous look on his face.

"I am going to be leaving tomorrow morning to go on vacation to Austin, Texas."

"What? Why are you going there? You don't know anyone in Austin?" I said back to him because I was stunned by his news. All these uneasy emotions inside of me started threatening to erupt. His nervous look was justified by how I was beginning to react towards him. I am not sure if I now had the same one on my face.

"I have a friend that I used to work with that lives there. He invited me to come and stay with him. I need to get away for a while."

"I don't believe he's just a friend!" I replied with an angry tone that shouldn't be in my voice, but it was.

"Yeah, I don't believe you and Cindy are just friends either!" he said sternly back to me as he turned his back on me and started to walk away.

"Wow, I know she and I are close, but we aren't more than friends. He must be jealous of her," I said to myself as he left my room.

He said goodbye to me before he left the next morning. I tried to sound like I wanted him to have a great trip when I told him that I hoped he would. I went outside after he left and sat alone on our patio. Sadness began to settle over me because I knew deep down that he had lied to me. He was off to spend the week with another man. I still had feelings for him that I didn't know I had.

Obviously, it seemed that he had finally let go of me to pursue someone else.

While my thoughts were taking my heart to a place it never wanted to go again, I was suddenly overcome by the presence of the Holy Spirit. I wasn't alone in my grief like I thought I was. I began experiencing Him in a way that I still struggle to describe to this day. He ministered to me in the sweetest, kindest, tenderest, most loving way anyone could ever imagine or hope to be. I started settling into this peace that passed my understanding.

When my ex-boyfriend returned from his trip, I suggested that we put our house up for sale. He didn't want us to sell the place. He angrily said it wasn't just my decision to make alone. He was right. He was willing to let go of me, but he wasn't ready to let go of his house. He had worked tirelessly to transform it into a place of beauty. He agreed to pay me back my half of the down payment money we used to purchase it. I would be taking a big financial hit, but I was convinced that was what was necessary for me to do.

I was sitting in his office at the bank where he worked. Tears began forming in his eyes as he handed me a cashier's check made out in the amount that we had agreed to before I signed the quit claim deed over to him. I was surprised by his tears. My heart started filling up with compassion for him. Somehow, I managed not to cry. That was unlike me, but I believed what we were doing was the best thing for both of us. I needed him to believe that too. My tears might have suggested that I was having second thoughts.

I began searching for an apartment. I needed one that could hold as much of the furniture that I owned, along with paintings, pictures, area rugs, and so forth. Cindy had a three-dimensional program on her computer that enabled her to input the measurements of an apartment space in order to see whether most of my stuff would fit into it. We finally found one that would do so.

I signed a one-year lease. Cindy directed the movers where to place the furniture in my apartment. She had already organized all of it on her computer program ahead of time, so she knew where it needed to go. Afterward, she hung up all my pictures and paintings for me. Her mother kindly set up my kitchen for me by organizing my cabinet space and drawers with dishes, silverware, pots and pans, and so forth. What a gift they both were at such a pivotal time in my life.

Cindy and I started dating. We were walking around at the Falls of the Ohio when I asked her if she would be my girlfriend. After we embraced and kissed each other, I felt heat on my back. It was weighty and intense. It was the Holy Spirit. He seemed to be affirming His approval of our decision to date each other. This was in a different way than He had ever manifested His presence to me. He might have been smiling more than either one of us.

Cindy and I went on a trip to Mexico. It was in late January 2014. My dad and stepmother were there also. As Cindy and I strolled down the beach holding hands, thoughts began stirring inside of me. I loved and adored her. So did some of my family members, especially my dad. Even though I had vowed never to get married again, I was beginning to be swayed on the inside to ask her to marry me. I was hesitant because I never wanted to hurt anyone else like I had hurt so many others in my past. I feared my past might repeat itself!

Once we got back from our trip, I couldn't get marriage out of my head or my heart. I went to a store that sold jewelry and began searching for an engagement ring. I found one that I liked and hoped she would like it as well. It was early in February. I decided that I would pop the question to her on the most romantic holiday of the year. On Valentine's Day, I would ask her to be my wife.

I waited for as long as I could after the lady at the store handed me the sales receipt. I think it was probably about thirty minutes before the ring and I were in my car heading to Cindy's apartment. I was disappointed when I got there because she wasn't at home. However, she pulled up in her car shortly after I had gotten there. I got out of my car as soon as I saw her get out of hers. She looked a little shocked to see me because we hadn't planned on getting together that particular night.

She opened her apartment door and walked inside. I hurried in behind her. She had been to the grocery store, and she had several bags in her hands. She was trying to make her way to the kitchen to set them down.

"I am surprised to see you," she said to me after she gave me a kiss.

I pushed her back gently away from me. She looked at me with a confused face.

"What's wrong? Is everything okay?" she asked.

"I was going to wait until Valentine's Day to ask you this, but I can't wait until then. I want us to get married. Will you marry me?" I asked as I pulled the ring out of my pocket.

"Are you sure that you want to get married?" she asked while she seemed to study my face to see if there might be any doubts lurking beneath the surface.

"Yes, I am sure," I said as convincingly as I could.

"Then yes, I will marry you," she said with a smile that indicated that she was happy while being surprised at the same time.

We had been dating for three years without any signs pointing towards something like this taking place.

I need to tell you that someone who was friends with both Cindy and I knew that I had cheated on her with some men. I had confessed to that person one night while we were out drinking together. I told them that my infidelity was the reason I was planning to break up with Cindy at that time. I believed that she should find someone else who wasn't a same-sex addict like me. I was drinking heavily almost every night too. This all happened after the church had kicked our ministry out of their building. I was disillusioned, to say the least. I thought, why should I bother fighting my desires when that's what happens when you tell the truth after a fall? I broke things off with Cindy for a while.

This particular friend and I were out having a drink together. Our conversation turned into a confrontation. It went something like this.

"Cindy and I are going to get married."

"You told me some time ago that she would be better off with someone else."

"Yes, but I love her, and she loves me."

They looked me in the eyes to make sure I didn't misunderstand what they were about to say next.

"If you don't tell her about how you cheated on her in the past, I will!"

I knew they were dead serious. It was apparent that they thought Cindy should know the truth before she made the worst mistake of her life by marrying someone like me. I knew I had to tell Cindy the truth before we moved forward with our wedding plans. Besides, it was best that she heard it from me and not someone else.

The next night, Cindy and I were sitting on her couch in her apartment. It was hard to look her in the face to tell her that I had been unfaithful to her, but I did. I braced myself for the worst after what had happened in the past when I told the truth. Oddly, she wasn't that surprised. She told me she had seen a shirtless picture of me wearing a cowboy hat on Halloween. It was apparent that I was in a bar because of what you could see in the background. One of my gay buddies had posted it on Facebook. I couldn't believe that he put that photo on there for all to see. I had contacted him in anger.

"What were you thinking posting on Facebook something like this?"

"I thought it was a good photo of you," he said while apologizing for doing so.

"Please take it down as soon as possible."

He agreed to remove it. The picture wasn't pulled down fast enough before she had viewed it. However, she had never confronted me about it.

She told me that she wasn't dumb. She already suspected that I had been unfaithful to her because of how I was half-naked in the pic. She had guessed that I was probably at a gay bar since my buddy was the one who posted it. Her intuition was correct. She told me that she still loved me anyway. I told her that I didn't blame her if she changed her mind about marrying me after my confession.

26

I was standing at the altar in a wedding chapel. I turned around as everyone behind me stood to their feet. There was music being played on a piano announcing that the bride-to-be was about to march. Cindy appeared in the doorway with her dad standing at her side. She was a vision dressed in a stunning white gown. Her beautiful smile wasn't hidden behind the veil she was wearing. I was mesmerized as I watched her take her first steps towards me. I already had butterflies in my stomach. They began fluttering around even more after I saw her. Tears began to surface as I tried to pull myself together. Once she and her dad reached the altar, he handed her off to me. Then, my vocal teacher broke out in song while she played effortlessly on the chapel's piano.

"And I have never been so sure of anything before like I am in this moment here with you."

She was singing "When I Say I Do." The song was written by Matthew West, who is a Christian recording artist. Later, she sang "Right Out of the Blue." The first song that I had ever written. She sang with such an anointing that morning.

The minister who performed our service was a dear friend of ours. He did an outstanding job of presenting the plan of marriage as instituted in Scripture by the Holy Spirit.

Many of our friends and family were there to witness this occasion. Most of them had prayed for a very long time for both of us.

Our wedding day was on July 5. We chose that date because it represented a time to celebrate our freedom. Yesterday, our nation celebrated its independence. Today, we were celebrating freedom from homosexuality. I believed that I would be free one day, but I believed that Cindy already was.

We vowed that we were determined to prayerfully see God's purposes for both of our lives fulfilled completely in our marriage to one another.

After we were pronounced husband and wife by the minister, everyone was invited to follow us outside. We were handed a white, wicker basket. With both of our hands on the lid, we slowly opened it up together. When we did so, two white doves began flapping their wings as they flew off together. This symbolized the Holy Spirit flying off with the two of us on our quest to do His will.

After the ceremony had ended, I thanked my vocal teacher for playing and singing for us. She said that it had been a blessing to be a part of what she had just witnessed.

"This is a miracle of God!" she exclaimed with an amazed look on her face that said more than her words ever could.

Our reception was held nearby, which made it convenient for everyone to stay and celebrate with us. I sang "Long as I Live" to Cindy before we toasted some sparkling grape juice together while standing in front of our wedding cake. Afterward, we made our way to each table to thank everyone for coming while they ate some delicious food that our caterer had prepared for the occasion.

We flew to Cancun, Mexico, for our honeymoon. The all-inclusive resort we stayed at was amazing. Our beautiful suite had a balcony that overlooked the breathtaking turquoise-blue water along the white sandy beach shoreline.

Our first day of celebration ended up with us in bed together. We were both nervous for different reasons. Cindy had never been with a man, and I hadn't slept with a woman in years. We were both smiling until the phonograph needle scratched across the romantic record playing in the background. Cindy wasn't able to have intercourse. She would later be diagnosed with atrophic vaginitis. I didn't know it at the time, so I assumed deep down that she must not be sexually attracted to me. That must be the real reason, I thought. We had waited to have sex with each other until we were married. Cindy will tell you that she was and is sexually attracted to her husband.

When we got back home, I headed out of town for training for my new job that I had landed. I was going to be gone from home for six weeks.

"God, we did what your Word says. We waited to have sex together until we got married. I didn't expect that we would start our marriage in the way things turned out in Mexico. Maybe we both just made one of the biggest mistakes of our lives?"

There was silence on the other end of the line.

I misperceived that Cindy had rejected me sexually. I was believing a lie. It set me up for my desires for men to come roaring back. I fell back into old sexual patterns again. It appeared that I hadn't changed even though I was married again. I became depressed and angry.

After I came back home from my training, I found out that I wasn't the only one feeling that way. My wife was feeling unwanted because of how her husband was emotionally distancing himself from her. She followed the doctor's protocol, and she was able to have intercourse. We consummated our marriage. However, my desires for men didn't go away.

One day, she came home to find me covered up in our bed. I was shivering with feverish symptoms. I had received an injection at the urgent care center near our home and was having a reaction to it. Based on the doctor's examination, she believed I had contracted a venereal disease. My blood test would later reveal a diagnosis of having contracted not one but two different STDs. One or more of my anonymous encounters had led to me getting the diseases.

Cindy sat down on the side of our bed. She gently put her hand on my shoulder.

"Greg, what's wrong? Why are you home from work this early?"

"I went to the doctor. They gave me a shot because they believed that I had an STD. I am sorry that I have obviously cheated on you. I never wanted to hurt you or anyone else, for that matter, ever again."

She responded very lovingly to me. She would later say that I must have been having sex with other people more than I was having it with her. She said that realization really hurt her. I had failed at being a faithful husband to my wife, just like I had in my first marriage. She did not divorce me even though she had a biblical right to do so. At that time, I believed that she should have ended our relationship then and there. She had a theological out. Her decision not to end it was based on what she had vowed on our wedding day, even though her husband had fallen short of his vows.

Would you have divorced me? Do you believe God should have ended His relationship with me too, based on what I have told you thus far? If you answered yes to either or both questions, I agree with you. I expected that both were going to leave me behind. Was it just a matter of time before that happened?

27

God had always dealt with me gently. I believe He did this because of how I had overreacted to things so many times in my life. He didn't want me to perceive that He was rejecting me because I was attracted to men.

I had believed that my father rejected me in his garage because he called me a sissy. I had felt rejected by many of the boys and girls who had called me by that name too. Looking back, I was only trying to act like my mom. I idolized her. I wanted to be just like her. By doing so, I was ridiculed by almost everyone in my life. At that time, I was confused by their verbal attacks. Now, I see things very differently.

Because of how my mother distanced herself from me, I believed that she no longer loved me like she once did.

How could she love a son who was gay?

She had told me that she was saddened by Rock Hudson after she found out about him. This was years before she knew anything about me being just like him.

"What a waste of a handsome man!" she had said to me.

I believed she must have felt the same way about me.

One day, the kid gloves came off God's hands.

"Greg, your life doesn't line up with what you say you believe. You are still having random encounters with men even though you aren't in a relationship with one. You are drinking almost every night to the point of getting drunk. You have a wife that you have hurt with your infidelity and your drunkenness. You aren't a spiritual leader. You have led her down a wrong path instead of a righteous one!" the Holy Spirit said.

"Your word says that Jesus will save me from my sins! I am still in them even though I have prayed many times to be saved from them!" I said back to Him.

He didn't say anything else back to me. I kept quiet too.

Not many days after, Cindy was gone out of town to visit a sick relative of hers who had been hospitalized. I was sitting outside on our patio listening to a recording of a minister who was full of the Holy Spirit. He had been radically saved and delivered from a drug addiction along with many other destructive patterns he couldn't overcome on his own. The Holy Spirit interrupted my thoughts about his testimony to inform me of some truths I desperately needed to hear.

"Do you know how Jesus was able to resist all of His temptations?" He asked.

"I guess because He had supernatural power even though He was in the flesh, right?" I responded.

"No, He had emptied Himself of His own deity being made in the likeness of sinful flesh. Paul wrote about this to the Philippians and the Romans. He resisted all of the devil's temptations by My power and not His own."

A light switch flipped to the on position inside of my heart. I was being shown a revelation about Jesus that I had never seen before. I had assumed things about Him that weren't true.

"So, that's how He can save me from my sins? His death on the cross empowered me to be saved from eternal death, which is the penalty for sin when I believed. I can be set free from the power of sin over me by faith. A faith that believes You will empower me in a way that will keep me from yielding to all temptations, including homosexual ones?" I asked.

He didn't have to answer me back because I knew what I was asking about was the truth. If you remember, the first cassette my counselor gave to me was about the book of Romans, where Paul said to reckon yourself dead to sin. He also says to kill the deeds of the body by the Spirit.

Suddenly, I understood that you do that by faith too. The writer of the book of Hebrews says that the just shall *live* by faith. Some of the other writers in the Bible say the exact same thing.

I understood that I hadn't been walking in the Spirit or even being led by Him. There's a verse in Romans that says that as many as are led by the Spirit, they are the sons of God. I began getting up every morning in faith and walking in the Spirit. I started having the power to resist my temptations. I was full of joy.

Shortly thereafter, I began writing this book that you are reading.

God cast a vision for a ministry called Unwanted Harvest.

Shortly thereafter, Cindy and I were invited to go to Dallas-Fort Worth to give our testimonies at a Christian conference. I planned on singing the song "Unwanted" that I had written right before I gave my testimony. I told Cindy that I planned to do so. She challenged me to find someone who could develop a musical track to accompany me. I was offended because I believed that she thought I didn't sing the song well enough a cappella. After I recovered from being offended, I took her advice and contacted my vocal teacher to see who she might recommend. I was able to meet with her recommendation in time to develop a track to take with me.

My dad and stepmom went to the conference to support us. It was a time of more healing with my dad. I told God that I was going to be honest and tell the truth instead of what people may have wanted to hear coming out of my mouth. I confessed to everyone there about my sexual falls and my excessive drinking, as well as other sins that I had been committing.

After I finished, a lady told me later that she had been in church for over thirty years and had never heard anyone give a testimony in the way that I did.

"I have never heard anything like this before. I cried the whole time you were talking."

"Thank you for letting me know. That makes me believe that I did what God had asked me to do. I believe everyone needs to get vulnerable and honest with each other. Drop our masks and tell the truth."

Later, a man came up and whispered in my ear.

"Don't feel guilty about your drinking. A.A. Allen had a drinking problem, but God did some mighty works through that evangelist!"

I tried to take comfort from what he told me, but I wasn't sure that I should.

A mutual friend of mine and Cindy's who was at the conference texted me after we got back home. She said that she was moved by how transparent I had been in telling my story. She said that it was a rare thing to witness. She thought that it shouldn't be. She said she also liked my "Unwanted" song that I sang.

In the book of James, he wrote that we should confess our sins to one another and pray for one another so that we may be healed. He wrote that under the inspiration of the Holy Spirit.

28

I was born cross-eyed. I wound up having two surgeries to try and correct the overactive muscle in my left eye. Over time, I developed a stigmatism in the same eye. My eyes never fused together. So, I have double vision, which causes me to look out of one eye instead of both. I favor the use of my *right* eye mostly.

Both of my spiritual eyes are *crossed* too. However, this *crossing* doesn't cause double vision. The vision they have is crystal clear about what Jesus accomplished for me on the cross.

I was lying in bed early one Sunday morning. Cindy was in our bathroom getting ready for church. I cannot tell you if I was dreaming or I beheld a vision. Either way, I saw Jesus hanging on the cross. I could somehow hear the sins of the whole world making an evil dissonance sound as they were making their presence known in the atmosphere all around Him. All at once, I felt all of them go into the body of Jesus. There wasn't a single one left in the air. Peaceful silence filled the empty space while fear filled my heart.

I raised up and tried to put my feet on the bedroom floor. My legs were weak, and I was trembling inside. So much that the insides of my chest were shaking uncontrollably. Somehow, I managed to reach our bathroom door. I opened it up and saw Cindy standing in front of the mirror, putting on her eye makeup. She turned to see that I was in great distress because of the look that she saw on my face.

"Greg, what's wrong with you?"

"It's gone. My homosexual sin is gone. So are all of my other sins," I said while trying to hold back the tears so I could tell her what just happened to me.

She started tearing up as she listened to what I was telling her.

"I just saw Jesus hanging on the cross. Every sin that I have committed or will ever commit went into His body."

I walked slowly over to where she was standing and put my arms around her. We both sobbed for quite some time. After composing myself emotionally, I turned and headed out of the bathroom into our living room.

I slowly sat down on our couch. I was still weak, and I hadn't quit shaking. The Bible talks about fear and trembling. This must have been what I was experiencing. I was undone. I was in awe of the power of God.

I had received revelation from the Holy Spirit about Him being able to give me the grace to overcome temptations of any kind. Now, I had seen a vision of the power of God. He had Jesus, who knew no sin, to become sin on my behalf. Surely, I would now walk in the Spirit and not fulfill the lusts of my flesh that Paul talks about in his letter to the Galatians?

29

I told you that I was getting up every day, and by faith, I was walking in the Spirit, but it didn't continue indefinitely. I got upset with God because I misperceived His timing regarding the vision of the ministry call on my life. Before I tell you about what happened because of my immaturity and ignorance, let me try to describe what it was like in the Spirit.

I had a joy that is unspeakable that Peter talks about in the Bible. I also had a peace that passed my understanding. I was in constant conversation with the Holy Spirit throughout my day. This was a two-way conversation.

My whole life was transformed. Cindy didn't recognize the man she was living with because I had dramatically changed. My job was transformed because I no longer looked at it as work. I believed that it was an opportunity to minister love and grace to my coworkers and the customers that I served on a daily basis. I had a supernatural energy that was difficult to describe as well. The joy of the Lord is my strength, was mentioned in the book of Nehemiah. I believe that was what I was experiencing.

As I walked around the retail store where I worked, the Holy Spirit would tell me mind-blowing revelations about many Scriptures that He had inspired to be written. He gave me an in-depth understanding about many topics, including sexuality and identity.

Amazing doesn't quite capture the place that I was in, but that's the only word that I think that comes close. Some things just have to be experienced in order to understand them. This is definitely one of those. David wrote in Psalm 34 to taste and see that the Lord is good. I agree wholeheartedly with King David.

As I said, I didn't stay in this place with God. I drifted back into the flesh. I wasn't continually being led by the Holy Spirit.

Therefore, I began falling back into familiar patterns of drinking and sexual sin.

Even though I may have had revelation and understanding, I had to maintain my faith and obedience to the Word.

According to the book of Jeremiah, the heart is more deceitful than all else and is desperately sick.

"Who can understand it?" Jeremiah asks.

My challenge was how to motivate myself to be obedient to what God says. Afterwards, to remain steadfast in being motivated daily.

I wasn't getting anything out of my sexual encounters, use of porn, drinking to excess, or any other sin for that matter.

"Why are you doing these things?" I asked myself.

I wasn't finding any pleasure in my sin, but I was still sinning.

In Hebrews, the writer talks about the pleasure of sin being for a season.

Any pleasure that I had in the past was gone. I was in a dilemma. I was caught in a cycle of perpetual falling without any stopping in sight.

30

In Genesis, Moses wrote to tell us that the fall of Adam was the result of a lie. Paul told us in Romans that man exchanged the truth of God for a lie.

My life had been full of so many lies.

I believed a lie that if I told people about my sexual desires, I would be rejected by everyone. I came out to my wife and my family. I told my secret on national television. No one close to me has rejected me.

I believed another lie that I was only going to be happy living in a loving relationship with a man. God allowed me to have a relationship that should have made me happy, but it didn't.

I believed a lie that God was going to leave me because of my sins. He didn't. He showed me that all of them were paid for on the cross with the blood of the Lamb (Jesus).

I believed that many in the church would reject me. Some did, but most did not. It was a lie.

I believed another lie that I would never preach or teach in church again. That was a lie because I have done both of them.

Another lie was that Christians were going to sin. *Surely, there must be certain sins that have power over each of us?* I believed that this must be true because the people who were telling me to stop sinning sexually hadn't repented of various sins in their own lives. It appeared to me that we are all going to be weak in some way, but we are forgiven, right? Aren't we saved even though we are sinning? This is one of the biggest deceptions that I think many in the church have believed today. John wrote in one of his letters that *if* you sin, you have an advocate with the Father, not *when* you sin.

The Holy Spirit is the Spirit of Truth. He guides us into all truth.

"You will *know* the truth, and the truth will *make* you free" (John 8:32, NASB), Jesus said, which is recorded for us in the gospel of John.

One day, I was outside on my patio. I was reading a Christian book when the Holy Spirit began speaking to me.

"Greg, there is a big difference between knowing about Me and really knowing Me personally. Singing about Me isn't singing for Me. You can deceive yourself by doing so-called ministry and assume that you are doing it for Me."

I was pierced in my heart with His words. I totally understood what He was telling me. I had begun my life with him at nineteen. My intentions were pure. I fell into sin. I left my first love. God was wooing me back to the beginning, back to the place where I left Him. Jesus warns us not to be deceived, but I have been. I believed that the deceptions came about by demonic influence. I believe that I had deceived myself also.

"I know what I need to do, God, but I am lacking the motivation to do it. I know You love me, but for some reason, I keep believing lies."

"I am glad you understand that it's lies that you are still believing. Your life reflects what you believe."

That stung, but I knew that He was telling me the truth. The truth that I needed to hear, whether I wanted to hear it or not. My life manifested exactly what I believed, whether I wanted to admit it or not.

31

When I returned from the Exodus conference in 2006, I had gone to a Christian bookstore. I was in search of trying to find a book that would help me overcome my homosexuality. I prayed to God to lead me to the right book. I left the store with a book named *Inside Out*. I was surprised that this was the book that the Holy Spirit wanted me to read.

It was a book that described what needs to occur in every believer. Paul writes in Romans about being predestined to be *conformed* to the image of the Son. He later writes in the same book that we are to be *transformed* by the renewing of our minds.

Another lie that I believed is that if my circumstances changed, then I would be happy. If I had the right person in my life, the right job, more money, a big house, a nice car, the ability to sing, and being in ministry, then I would be happy. I thought that if things on the outside were perfect, then I would change inwardly as well. Paul told the Philippians that he learned to be content in whatever circumstances he faced.

One day, the Holy Spirit spoke to me. This time, He was more serious in His tone than He had ever been with me.

"Greg, you do understand that We are eternal?"

"Yes, I do believe that, God."

"There is a reason that We are eternal. It is because of Our attributes. We are holy and righteous. There is not an ounce of sin in any of Us. The only way you are going to be eternal is to become like Us. Do you understand what I am saying to you? You must become one with Us. Jesus prayed to the Father that you would be one with Us."

"I know that passage of Scripture. I have meditated on it. I also know the one where Jesus said that this is eternal life that they may *know* You, the only true God, and Jesus Christ whom You have sent."

"If you don't become one with Us, you won't have eternal life."

He had my full attention. I began to understand the fear of the Lord that day. I no longer wanted to be separated from Him by my sin. I wanted to be sober-minded and continually walk with Him. Now, I feared to be away from Him.

Another time that God spoke to me, I was reading a Christian book about sonship. The Holy Spirit interrupted my reading.

"I gave you the father that you have. You weren't born into your family by some sort of accident. I chose him for you and you for him."

I was shell-shocked. I quickly began seeing my dad in a different light.

"Thank You for giving me a dad who would pray for me without ceasing. One who would love me regardless of my shortcomings or how I may have embarrassed him," I responded with tears welling up.

Immediately, I picked up the phone and called my dad. I was happy that he answered my call. I began crying and telling him how much I loved him. I thanked him for loving me and for praying all of the years that he had for me. It was the most powerful time of healing when he and I were concerned. I believe he experienced some of his own healing during our conversation.

I hadn't shared with you an earlier time when the Holy Spirit was able to get in my face about my father. Now would be the time to tell you. It went something like this.

"Greg, I know you have read that you became a homosexual because of a passive father who you believed rejected you."

"Yes, I definitely agree that is one of the factors that caused me to *be gay."*

"*You rejected your father before he ever rejected you. You sized him up as weak because you believed that he let your mom control him. You vowed that you were never going to be like him or any other man. You were determined that you weren't going to be controlled by anyone.*"

I was stunned by what I was hearing. He was uncovering my hidden pride. It was tough to look at the truth.

Malachi tells us that God is going to send Elijah, the prophet, before the coming of the great and terrible day of the Lord. He will restore the hearts of the fathers to their children and the hearts of the children to their fathers so that God will not come and smite the land with a curse.

God restored the heart of my father to me and my heart to my father. It was something that only He could have done.

I wrote a song called "The Man I Wanted to Be." I believe that all the songs that I wrote on the *Unwanted* CD were prophetic. This one is about my dad and I. The rejection that I felt. The hatred I had in my heart for him. In the chorus, it says, "I didn't know hating you, I'd be losing me."

God showed me some ways that I am like my dad. By rejecting him, I was rejecting parts of myself. By vowing never to be like my dad or other weak men, I had disconnected from my own masculinity. By the time I hit puberty, my identity as someone different than my dad or other men was solidified.

There are studies that indicate what we believe can change our DNA. I do not claim to be an expert, but I have read about it. The Bible says in Proverbs, as a man thinks in his heart, so is he. Again, we believe with our hearts. Another way of saying this is what we believe on the inside will manifest itself on the outside (*Inside Out*).

In the bridge of the song, it says, "Look now embracing me, the man I wanted to be, I'm the man I wanted to be." I believe I am becoming the man that I want to be. That man is the man that God created me to be in my mother's womb. Nothing more or nothing less than him is my heart's desire.

The understanding that I had about Jesus being the Son of man who was sent to the earth by God the Father gave me hope that I could fulfill the will of the Father just like Him. He did it by the power of the Holy Spirit. He said that we will do the works that He has done and even greater works. I can be a son in whom He is well pleased.

32

One day, I was working out at the gym when I realized that I had lost my cell phone. I didn't panic. I started retracing my steps. I went to the first place I had been to, and it wasn't there. Then, I remembered I had been using the leg press machine.

It probably fell out of my pocket when I was working out on it, I thought to myself.

When I got there, I saw that it was lying on the floor next to the machine. As I bent down to pick it up, God spoke to me.

"When you lose something, you must go back to the place you lost it," the Holy Spirit said to me.

At that moment, I realized that He had been taking me back to the places in my life where I had lost my faith, and at other places where I had lost my masculinity.

In the past, I had been able to believe that God was able to do mighty things in others' lives but not my own. I was ambivalent in my belief. Was my ambivalence a state of doublemindedness? I believe my head wanted to believe, but my heart really didn't. In the Bible, James says that a double-minded man is unstable in all of his ways.

In fairness to myself, I was confused about where God and my sexuality were concerned. I prayed to Him about changing me, but He didn't. Can you pray the gay away? It didn't appear so in my life, but now I am convinced that you can *believe* it away by faith.

The book of Hebrews reminded me that the children of Israel didn't enter the promised land because of their unbelief. I was no longer dying in my unbelief, but I was living by faith.

The book of Revelation was written by John for seven different churches. One of those was Laodicea. This church was told by

Jesus that they believed they had no need of anything, but He told them that they do not know that they are *wretched* and *miserable* and *poor* and *blind* and *naked*. I was in the same condition. Jesus revealed to me that I would be spit out of his mouth just like they would be unless I repented.

On another occasion, I listened to a testimony from a pastor in Africa. This man had preached for many years. He had seen signs and wonders performed during his ministry. The presence of God had come upon him in such a way that he couldn't move his body. His tongue cleaved to the roof of his mouth so he couldn't speak. God began speaking to his heart.

"If I came for my bride today, I wouldn't take you," the Holy Spirit told him.

Then he showed him his sins, how he had been on platforms preaching while having lust in his heart. He revealed other things his evil heart was doing. He became very afraid. He knew that he had been deceived. He repented.

My name, Gregory, means watchman. Ezekiel is told by God that He had appointed him as a watchman to the house of Israel. He said I had made your face like flint.

"When I say to the wicked, you will surely die, and you do not warn him or speak out to warn the wicked from his wicked way that he may live, that wicked man shall die in his iniquity, but his blood I will require at your hand. Yet, if you have warned the wicked and he does not turn from his wickedness or from his wicked way, he shall die in his iniquity, but you have delivered yourself" (Ezekiel 3:18–19, NASB), God told Ezekiel.

I am in no way putting myself as a watchman over anyone. However, I believe that by writing this book, I am warning many souls about the deception they may have believed. God told me to write this book. In writing this book out of obedience, I do not have anyone's blood on my hands.

One day, the Holy Spirit was talking to me about the current state of many churches in the United States and other parts of the world.

"Remember when hospice came to your parents' home to assist your mother in dying?" He asked me.

"Yes, I remember. I was thankful for the nurse who was there to help her. She kept my dad informed on how my mom was doing. She alerted him to call all of the kids to let us know that her passing was close at hand. We made it just in time to their house before she died," I said with a puzzled look on my face because I didn't know where He was headed in our conversation.

"There are church leaders who are deceived, and thus, they are deceiving their congregations. They are like hospice nurses. They are making their members as comfortable and pain-free as possible before they are ushered into eternal destruction."

I gasped. His revelation shook me to my core. Then, righteous anger rose inside me. Paul wrote to Timothy that in the last days, many shall depart from the faith, giving heed to seducing doctrines (teachings) of devils. I understood how I had departed from the faith, but now I was back in the fight again.

In the book of Matthew, Jesus is quoted saying, "Not everyone who says to Me, Lord, Lord, will enter the kingdom of heaven, but he who does the will of My Father who is in heaven will enter. Many will say to Me on that day, Lord, Lord, did we not prophesy in Your name, and in Your name cast out demons, and in Your name perform many miracles? And then I will declare to them, I never knew you, depart from Me, you who practice lawlessness" (Matthew 7:21–23, NASB).

In my opinion, this is one of the most bone-chilling Scriptures in the Bible.

In the book of Luke, it talks about the seventy returning with joy, saying, "Lord, even the demons are subject to us in Your name"

(Luke 10:17, NASB).

Jesus says a few verses later for them not to rejoice in the authority that they have been given. The authority that the spirits are subject to you, but rejoice that your names are recorded in heaven.

33

God has been so patient with me. I don't think that I would have been likewise with someone like myself. Nevertheless, He has been. All of His actions towards me have been loving. I will forever be grateful and thankful to Him for telling me His truth.

One of the most sobering statements that He recently said to me was an eye-opener.

"Greg, either you *destroy* your flesh, or it's going to *destroy* you. There isn't such a thing as neutral ground. You are either for Me or against Me. You must not only love righteousness but hate sin. I hate sin not only because it separated you from Me, but because it will destroy you in the end."

I didn't have to respond back to Him. He knew that I understood Him. My heart shifted from being casual to being more serious than I had ever been. He had sobered me up.

I meditated on His words. The book of James's Scripture came up in my spirit.

But each one is tempted when he is carried away and enticed by his own lust. Then, when lust has conceived, it gives birth to sin, and when sin is accomplished, it brings forth death.

The *flesh* is our sinful nature that we all have because of Adam. Paul speaks explicitly about it in his letter to the Galatians. We are at the mercy of our flesh. Another way to describe it would be that we are in bondage. We are slaves to sin (sinners).

When we believe in Jesus, we are born again. He is called the last Adam by Paul. Immediately, the Holy Spirit enters us because we are cleansed by the blood of the Lamb. Now, we are the temple of the Holy Spirit. The flesh is still residing in our bodies, though. Thus, a war between the flesh and the Spirit starts.

If we, by faith, follow the leading of the Spirit, we will destroy the works of the flesh in our lives.

According to Paul, the works or deeds of the flesh are *immorality*, impurity, sensuality, idolatry, sorcery, enmities, strife, jealousy, outbursts of anger, disputes, dissensions, factions, envying, drunkenness, carousing, and things like these. He warned the Galatians that those who practice such things will not inherit the kingdom of God.

Peter wrote to tell us that as obedient children, do not be conformed to the passions of your former *ignorance*, but as He who called you is holy, you also be holy in your conduct, since it is written, "You shall be holy, for I am holy" (1 Peter 1:16, NASB).

If you are like I was, you are saying that God is asking us to do something that is impossible! You are correct in believing that you and I cannot do the impossible, but God in us can.

One of the songs that I wrote on the Unwanted CD is "All Things Possible." The message of this song is that all things are possible *if you believe*. It talks about the fact that God's arm is not too short to save. Nothing is too hard for Him. The same God who made a virgin to give birth, who turned water into wine, will do the impossible for you if you believe.

The writer of the Hebrews told us that without *faith*, it is impossible to please Him, for he who comes to God must *believe* that He is and that He is a rewarder for those who seek Him.

If you remember, I told you that one of the churches I attended supposedly cast seven demons out of me. I didn't feel any different afterward.

I heard a well-known Christian speaker and author say that God told him that you cannot cast out the *flesh*. He said that the *flesh* must be crucified.

Paul told the Galatians that those who belong to Christ Jesus have crucified the *flesh* with its passions and desires. I believe this verse gives meaning to when Jesus said, "If anyone wishes to come after Me, he must deny himself, and take up his cross and follow Me" (Mark 8:34, NASB). This is not optional. It is something every believer *must* do.

In other words, we must all be led *by the Spirit* into a place that's like the garden of Gethsemane. Gethsemane means oil press. This is where Jesus sweat drops of blood while praying to His Father the night before He was crucified. We must go through a similar crushing of our wills. We must hear the Father tell us that it isn't possible for the crucifixion of our flesh to pass from us. There's no other way. It's the *only* way. We must say, "Not my will, but Yours be done."

If you have read the Bible, you may recall how John describes the scene where Jesus is telling Peter in the way he was going to be martyred.

> Truly, truly, I say to you, when you were younger, you used to gird yourself and walk wherever you wished; but when you grow old, you will stretch out your hands and someone else will gird you, and bring you where you do not wish to go. Now this He said, signifying by what kind of death he would glorify God. And when He had spoken this, He said to him, "Follow Me!"
>
> John 21:18–19 (NASB)

Jesus is commanding everyone who believes in Him to follow Him by crucifying their flesh. We must see the flesh as an enemy that must be destroyed before it destroys us. We do this by grace through faith with the Holy Spirit. Jesus did it the same way. He was the Son of Man who was full of the Holy Spirit.

The writer of Hebrews said, "Looking unto Jesus the author and finisher of our faith; who for the joy that was set before Him endured the cross, despising the shame, and is set down at the right hand of the throne of God" (Hebrews 12:2, KJV).

Finally, Paul said to the Galatians, "I have been crucified with Christ and it is no longer I who live, but Christ lives in me; and the life which I now live in the flesh I live by *faith* in the Son of God, who loved me and gave Himself up for me. I do not nullify the grace of God, for if righteousness comes through the Law, then Christ died needlessly" (Galatians 2:20–21, NASB).

The good news is because of Jesus, everyone who believes can lay down their own wills and take up the Father's will. We can accomplish all that He is asking us to do by the power of the Holy Spirit, just like His Son did. All hell may, and probably will, try to stop us, but they can't. The demonic realm no longer has the power or the authority to do so. The only thing that can stop us is our *unbelief!*

34

I have a friend who is a member of the same church Cindy and I attend. We were at her house around six years ago. She was hosting a gathering of believers for prayer. I asked her and the others who were in attendance to pray about this book you are reading.

After the prayer ended, this lady looked at me to tell me that she had experienced a vision while praying.

"This book is going to be written for multitudes of people. I saw all of these men and women that it is going to reach for the kingdom of God."

I was overwhelmed by what she had just said to me.

Then, her husband spoke up.

"I saw you riding on a horse back and forth in front of a large group of people who were also mounted on their horses."

When he said this, the scene from "Braveheart" came into my mind. William Wallace, played by Mel Gibson, was on a horse in front of an army saying this speech.

"Aye, fight and you may die. Run and you'll live, for at least a while. And dying in your beds many years from now, would you be willing to trade all the days from this day to that for one chance, just one chance to come back here and tell our enemies that they may take our lives, but they'll never take our freedom!"

It was a very powerful moment in Scottish history.

"I saw a platform and a microphone. I don't know if you sing, but it starts here," her son said to me.

I have only ridden a horse a couple of times in my life, but I have been up behind a microphone numerous times singing, testifying and preaching.

Paul said in the Bible that our war is not against flesh and blood, but against the rulers, against the authorities, against the powers of this dark world, and against the spiritual forces of evil in the heavenly realms.

John wrote about Jesus, saying that if the Son makes you free, you will be free indeed.

Right after the 2020 presidential election results, I became very upset about the outcome. I was fearful that the freedom that we were given by our constitution was going to be taken away from us.

"God, the blood of the men and women who have died so that we can have our freedom is going to be in vain!"

"Yes, perhaps, but what about the blood My Son shed? The deception and unbelief of so many today are causing His death to be in vain. He died so that many will believe and thus have freedom from sin and death, but many are blinded and can't see the truth. Others are refusing to believe it!"

Ouch! I was more concerned about the things of the world instead of having an eternal perspective. I was having righteous anger, which is a good thing. However, I should be more upset by the great deception that grips so many by the proverbial throat. It is choking out the eternal life that Jesus died for them to have.

In Matthew, he wrote about Jesus saying to not fear those who kill the body but are unable to kill the soul; rather, fear Him who is able to destroy both body and soul in hell fire.

Paul wrote to Timothy saying that I am already being poured out like a drink offering, and the time of my departure has come. I have fought a good fight, I have finished my course, *I have kept the faith*; in the future there is laid up for me a crown of righteousness, which the Lord, the righteous Judge, will award me on that day; not only to me, but also to all who have loved His appearing (1 Timothy 4:6–8, NASB).

The United States is experiencing something similar to what

Paul calls a great falling away in his second letter to the Thessalonians. We are a country that was founded on Christian principles. Some have fallen away from (abandoned) these principles, along with trying to undermine the very foundation our country was built upon. That is our constitution.

I am not writing this chapter to be political. I believe the year 2020 was one that should have brought the condition of our country into a clearer vision for all of us to see. Not just our country, though. The whole world is in chaos.

I believe that we are in the *last* of the last days. I am not predicting the day nor the hour that Jesus is returning, but the signs are shouting at us. Some have deaf ears and do not hear what the Spirit is saying to them.

Matthew quoted Jesus saying, "Therefore be on alert, for you do not know which day your Lord is coming" (Matthew 24:42, NASB).

Paul wrote to the Romans, saying, "Do this *knowing the time*, that it is already the hour for you to awaken from sleep; for now, salvation is nearer to us than when we believed. The night is almost gone, and the day is near. Therefore, let us lay aside the deeds of darkness and put on the armor of light. Let us behave properly as in the day, not in carousing and drunkenness, not in sexual promiscuity and sensuality, not in strife and jealousy. But put on the Lord Jesus Christ, and make no provision for the flesh in regard to its lusts" (Romans 13:11–14, NASB).

The godly alarm has sounded. We have received a wakeup call!

Repent and become sober-minded unless you have already.

35

My rollercoaster ride with homosexuality has come to a screeching halt. I have begun to hate this sin. It separated me from the man I was created to be. I am filled with mixed emotions at this point in my life.

I believe that we are all born with the disease of sin. Sin is manifested in a variety of symptoms. Many in the church thought my symptom of homosexuality was somehow worse than their symptoms. The last time I checked, the Bible says the wages of *sin* is death. It doesn't single out anywhere in the Bible that homosexual acts are the worst kind of sin, but let's look at what it does say.

Before we look, I want to point out something that I believe is true. Paul, in his letter to the Galatians, said that the Law has become a tutor to lead us to Christ, so that we may be justified by faith. In other words, the Law was given to alert us to the condition of sin that we all have because of Adam. God was gracious to show us that we all have something that is destroying us. We are incapable of overcoming it by ourselves.

If He had removed my same-sex desires (symptom), I wouldn't have known that there was something deeper inside me that needed His healing. I had been separated from my masculine identity very early in my life. I needed to believe that God had the power to restore what had been lost. He is mighty to save, and He has the power to restore all things back to Himself!

Let's look at Genesis, where Moses wrote about the destruction of Sodom and Gomorrah.

Two angels, who appeared as men, came towards the city of Sodom. Lot was sitting at the gate and went to meet them. They told him that they were going to spend the night in the square. Lot strongly urged them not to do so. They accepted his hospitality and entered his house.

A feast was offered to them along with baked unleavened bread, and they ate. Before they laid down, the men of Sodom surrounded the house, both young and old, all the people from every quarter, and they called to Lot and said to him, "Where are the men who came to you tonight? Bring them out to us that we might have relations with them" (Genesis 19:5, NASB). But Lot went out to them at the doorway, shut the door behind him, and said, "Please do not act wickedly. Now behold, I have two daughters who are virgins, let me bring them out to you to do whatever you like with them; only do nothing to these men, inasmuch as they have come under the shelter of my roof" (Genesis 19:7–8, NASB).

This is just an excerpt of this story in Genesis 19. Does God want us to believe this is a story about hospitality or one about attempted homosexual gang rape? Lot's offer of his two daughters suggests that he believed that homosexual rape would be worse than heterosexual rape. I believe both kinds of rape are condemned.

In his letter to the Romans, Paul wrote that by believing a lie, some exchanged natural sexual functions for unnatural ones. Women burning in their lusts for other women, and men burning in their lusts for other men. These received in their own persons the due penalty for their error. I believe they were sexually hooked in a bondage that they would remain in unless Someone more powerful than themselves came and led them out of it.

In Leviticus 18, Moses wrote that you shall not lie with a male as one lies with a female; it is an abomination. This chapter also decrees that incest of any kind is forbidden, along with bestiality and lusting after your neighbor's wife. The judgment for whoever does any of these abominations; those persons who do so shall be cut off from among their people. So, any acts of sexual immorality, including homosexual acts, resulted in being stoned to death.

Does the Bible specifically say anything about the sin of Sodom? Yes, it speaks about the sins of Sodom in the book of Ezekiel (chapter 16).

> Behold, this was the guilt of your sister Sodom; she and her daughters had arrogance (pride), abundant food and careless ease, but she did not help the poor or needy. Thus, they were haughty (prideful) and committed abominations before Me. Therefore, I removed them when I saw it.
>
> Ezekiel 16:49–50 (NASB)

Were some of the abominations, homosexual acts, or homosexual gang rape? I heard a well-known speaker talk about the four cities that God destroyed by fire and brimstone. They were Sodom, Gomorrah, Adman, and Zeboiim. He said each of these cities had a judge who passed a law that a bed could be put in their streets. If a foreigner came into their cities, the men could stretch them out on these beds and rape (sodomize) them. This is reported in chapter nineteen of the book of Jasher. Based on this information, I believe it's saying that the men of Sodom raped strangers who entered their cities.

The story says that the men of Sodom rejected Lot's offer to do whatever they wanted to his two virgin daughters. They pressed hard against Lot and came near to break down the door. But the men (angels) reached out their hands and brought Lot into the house with them and shut the door. They struck the men who were at the doorway of the house with blindness, both small and great so that they wearied themselves trying to find the doorway.

If you remember, one of the things Jesus told the church at Laodicea was that they were blind. Sodom had abundant food and careless ease. Laodicea believed they were in need of nothing. *Pride* blinds us from the truth.

In the story of Samson in the book of Judges, the first thing his enemy did after all of Samson's Nazirite vows were broken was put out his eyes (blinded him).

In the second letter to the Corinthian church, Paul wrote the god (Satan) of this world has blinded the minds of the unbelieving so that they might not see the light of the gospel of the glory of Christ, who is the image of God. He had told them in his first letter that the word of the cross is foolishness to those who are perishing, but to us who are being saved, it is the power of God. For it is written, "I will destroy the wisdom of the wise, and the cleverness of the clever I will set aside" (1 Corinthians 1:19, NASB).

My conclusion is that homosexual acts between two people as well as homosexual rape are sinful. Both are condemned, and they result in a penalty of eternal destruction.

Paul's first letter to the Corinthians states that the unrighteous will not inherit the kingdom of God. He said, "do not be *deceived*; neither fornicators, nor idolaters, nor effeminate, nor *homosexuals*, nor thieves, nor the covetous, nor drunkards, nor revilers, nor swindlers, will inherit the kingdom of God. Such were some of you, but you were *washed*, but you were *sanctified*, but you were *justified* in the name of the Lord Jesus Christ and *in the Spirit* of our God" (1 Corinthians 6:9–11, NASB).

I had been guilty of most of the actions of the people who were not going to be inheriting the kingdom of God, including homosexual acts. The good news for me is that I have been washed by the Word of God. I have also been washed by the blood of the Lamb. The Spirit of God has sanctified me, which means to be set apart, declared holy and consecrated. All of this has been done through *faith*.

36

Moses wrote in Genesis that God destroyed everyone except for Noah and his family by a flood. Noah was a righteous man, blameless in his time; Noah walked with God.

At that time, the earth was corrupt in the sight of God, and the earth was filled with violence. The Lord saw that the wickedness of man was great on the earth and that every intent of the thoughts of his heart was only evil continually. The Lord was sorry that He had made man on the earth, and He was grieved in His heart.

Hebrews says that, "By *faith* Noah, being warned by God about things not yet seen, in reverence prepared an ark for the salvation of his household, by which he condemned the world, and became an heir of the righteousness which is according to *faith*" (Hebrews 11:7, NASB).

God destroyed all of mankind off the face of the earth. One of the symptoms of the wickedness was that violence filled the earth. Does that sound anything like what is being manifested in America? The burning of some of our major cities by violent protestors, violent attacks by mobs, violent attacks against police officers and other authorities, mass shootings at schools and universities, and the list goes on and on.

Our land isn't the only one experiencing violence. It is global. There are wars going on and rumors of possible wars. Nuclear war seems imminent by some of the reports that we are hearing.

Luke wrote in his gospel about Jesus talking about His coming. It will be just as fast as lightning flashing across the sky. His coming will take many by surprise. Jesus told us it would be just like in the days of Noah and in the days of Sodom. People will be conducting their lives with business as usual before sudden destruction has come upon them. Jesus goes on to give us a warning. Remember Lot's wife. When the two angels took Lot and his family by the hand to lead them out of Sodom, they instructed all of them not to look back. Lot's wife didn't heed their instructions. She looked back and was turned into a pillar of salt.

Repentance is the only thing that's going to stop God from sending Jesus to end the world as we know it.

An unwilling prophet named Jonah was sent to deliver a message to Nineveh. The message was that God was going to overthrow (destroy) their city in forty days. The king and his nobles heeded the warning by issuing a decree. "Do not let man, beast, herd, or flock taste a thing. Do not let them drink water. Both man and beast must be covered with sackcloth; and let men call on God earnestly that each man may turn from his wicked way and from the violence which is in his hands. Who knows, God may turn and relent and withdraw His burning anger so that we will not perish. When God saw their deeds, that they turned from their wicked way, then God relented concerning the calamity which He had declared he would bring upon them." This is found in Jonah 3:7–10 (NASB).

He did not destroy them because they had humbled themselves in their repentance.

37

One night, my first wife had a dream. She saw me in a barred cell. I was cowered down in the corner, trembling in fear. There was a big angel with wings standing beside me. He was looking down over me. The strange thing was the prison door was wide open.

Finally, I understand the interpretation of this dream. I was free, but I was too afraid to walk out of my cell. So, I stayed for years in a place I didn't want to be in, but I was too scared to leave.

Most, if not all of us, are afraid of the unknown. The nation of Israel had been enslaved in Egypt for four hundred and thirty years. They cried out unto God to save them. He sent Moses after He heard their cries.

Moses led them into the wilderness. There, they walked around for forty years. They feared the giants that inhabited the land they had been promised by God. They were unbelieving that God would deliver them, even though they watched Pharoah and his army drown in the Red Sea. They died in the wilderness and never entered the Promised Land.

I am not scared anymore. I am full of faith in believing that what God has promised me, He is able to deliver. Jesus destroyed the enemy of our souls with His red blood. He can destroy the fleshly nature that we inherited from Adam if only we *believe* that He can.

I do not have a doctorate degree in theology or psychology. I am just someone who has walked on and off with God for over forty-plus years now. I am turning sixty-three years old this coming August. God has answered most of my questions about one of the symptoms of my sinful nature that I have battled. I have experienced that when you say *no* to one of your symptoms, another one attempts to rise up. That's why our flesh must be crucified.

If I hadn't struggled with such a stigmatized sin, I don't believe I would know God in the way that I have come to know Him. If I had a more acceptable sin (there's not such a thing where God is concerned) that the majority of people struggle with, then I would probably still be the self-righteous hypocrite that I used to be years ago.

I love what Luke wrote in the book of Acts 4. Now, as they observed the confidence of Peter and John and understood that they were uneducated and untrained men, they were amazed and began to recognize them as having been with Jesus. I hope you can see that I have been with Him too.

My prayer is that God has been with you on this ride that you took with me. I believe that some of you may struggle with the same sin that I have. Some of you may have with other issues. None of us are unwanted by God. Now, the only thing that is unwanted in my life is sin. I am hungering and thirsting after righteousness.

John wrote in his gospel that Jesus is the Word of God who became flesh and dwelt among us. In Psalm 107:20 (NASB) says, "He sent His word and healed them, and delivered them from their destructions." Jesus healed all who came to Him and believed. He has healed me of many things. I told you about Crohn's disease already.

Let me share with you about the time He healed me instantly. I was at work and started having some distressing symptoms. I have an enlarged prostate, and I thought that it was causing me the discomfort that I was experiencing. I left work and headed home.

By the time I got to our house, my symptoms had worsened. I went to the bathroom and started throwing up. I began to think that maybe I was under a demonic attack of some sort. The reason I thought this might be possible was because our church was having a revival service that night. I didn't want to miss it. I believed the devil didn't want me to go. Anger and faith rose inside of me.

Even though Cindy was just on the other side of the house, I texted her. I was too sick to walk to her office, where she was working. I asked her to please come to our bathroom.

"Greg, what's wrong? Why did you text me?"

"I am sick, and I want you to pray for me. The Holy Spirit is telling me that you should come against a spirit of infirmity."

She laid her hands on me and began to pray. As she came against the spirit of infirmity, a warmth started rising inside me. It was different than what I had ever experienced before with the Holy Spirit. The heat began filling my entire body but stopped before it entered an area in my lower back. I heard the Holy Spirit say to tell Cindy to pray for my kidneys. I told her what He said. As soon as the words came out of her mouth, the heat filled me completely. All of my symptoms were gone. I was healed. This only took a couple of minutes or less to happen. I smiled and told Cindy that I was healed. I thanked her for praying for me. I thanked God for healing me. We were at the revival meeting later that night.

I had called my urologist and set up an appointment with him when my symptoms first started. This was before Cindy had prayed for me. I was sitting in his office the next day after I had been healed.

"What brings you in to see me?"

"I was having some uncomfortable pain. I was nauseous, which caused me to vomit a few times. Also, my urine was brown."

"Are you still having any symptoms? It sounds like a kidney stone."

"No. My wife prayed for me. The symptoms have subsided."

"Well, tell your wife to keep praying for you. I want to have a CT scan setup to make sure that you passed the stone," he said while smiling about Cindy praying for me."

The scan showed that I had very small residual stones. The Holy Spirit had busted up a larger one, and the residual proof was all that remained.

In the gospel of Mark, a blind beggar named Bartimaeus cried out to Jesus when he heard that He was passing by. He said, "Jesus, Son of David, have mercy on me!" Many were sternly telling him to be quiet, but he kept crying out all the more, "Son of David have mercy on me!" And Jesus stopped and said, "Call him here." So, they called the blind man, saying to him, "Take courage, stand up! He is calling for you." Throwing aside his cloak, he jumped up and came to Jesus. And answering him, Jesus said, "What do you want me to do for you?" And the blind man said to Him, "Rabbi, I want to regain my sight!" And Jesus said to him, "Go, your *faith* has made you well." Immediately, he regained his sight and began following Him on the road.

I was like blind Bartimaeus. I couldn't see because of my pride. My *faith* in God has made me well. Now I can see!

Paul wrote in his second letter to the Corinthians that God was in Christ, reconciling the world to Himself, not counting their trespasses against them, and He has committed to us the word of reconciliation.

Peter wrote in his second letter that the Lord is not slow about His promise, as some count slowness, but is patient toward you, not wishing for *any* to perish but for *all* to come to repentance.

God created the heavens and the earth, according to Moses, who wrote the book of Genesis. He created Adam and Eve. King David said that God formed him in his mother's womb. That means that God formed you and me in our mother's wombs too. None of us are here by accident.

Like me, you may have felt unwanted for some reason. There are numerous reasons why we might feel that way. However, you are one of a kind. There's no one else like you. No one else has your fingerprints, your voice, your face, or your personality. You are uniquely you.

Right now, you might be saying, "Greg, you don't know where I have been or what has happened to me!"

You're right. I don't, but I know Someone who does. He went through a scandal regarding His birth because His mother was a virgin. He was rejected by the people He was sent to save. One of his friends betrayed Him. Some witnesses falsely accused Him. Then, He was beaten thirty-nine times with a whip that had bits of iron and/or bone attached to the strips of leather. Each time He was struck, it would have torn into His flesh. Afterward, He had to carry His heavy cross up Golgotha's hill. There, Roman soldiers stripped Him naked and stretched Him out on the wood as they hammered nails through His hands and feet. One of the soldiers placed a crown of thorns on His head. Then, they lifted Him up on the cross and dropped it into a hole. His mother was there and watched Him as He fulfilled the prophecy that had been told to her by the angel Gabriel thirty-three years earlier. His Father turned away, it seems, because Jesus cried out, "My God, My God, why have You forsaken Me?" Just before He took His last breath, He declared, "It is finished!" He had fulfilled His Father's will. He died. He was buried in a tomb with a large stone placed at the entrance. On the third day, an angel rolled that stone away. Jesus was alive again, and He walked out of His grave. However, our sins remained buried there forever!

Isaiah wrote, " He was despised and forsaken of men, a man of sorrows and acquainted with grief; and like one from whom men hide their face. He was despised and we did not esteem Him. Surely our griefs He Himself bore, and our sorrows He carried; yet we ourselves esteemed Him stricken, smitten of God and afflicted" (Isaiah 53:3–4, NASB). He wrote that passage around seven hundred years *before* Jesus was executed on the cross.

Shortly after I had moved to Louisville, I met a man who had been delivered from his homosexuality. He was leading an ex-gay ministry. In our conversation together, I asked him this question.

"Why did you want to stop being gay?"

"I chose life," He said to me.

I was puzzled by his response, but now I understand that he was referring to a verse from Deuteronomy that Moses wrote.

"I call heaven and earth to witness against you today, that I have set before you, life and death, blessing and the curse. So, choose life in order that you may live, you and your descendants, by loving the Lord your God, by obeying His voice, and by holding fast to Him; for this is your life and the length of your days, that you may live in the land which the Lord swore to your fathers, to Abraham, Isaac, and Jacob, to give them" (Deuteronomy 30:19–20, NASB).

You may have heard it said that life is short, so live it to the fullest. I say, eternal life never ends, so strive to obtain it. Many are trading eternity for a few years here on this earth. Some may live to be eighty or even a hundred years old. What is that compared to a life that is never going to end?

James wrote that you are just a vapor that appears for a little while and then vanishes away.

Solomon wrote in the book of Ecclesiastes that God has made everything appropriate in its time. He has also set eternity in their heart. I believe that means that we can *believe* in eternal life.

Paul wrote in his letter to the Romans that God has allotted to each a measure of faith. In the first part of this same letter, he wrote God's eternal power and divine nature have been clearly seen, being understood through what has been made so that we are without excuse.

I am going to sing the last chorus of the "Unwanted" song that I wrote for you.

Unwanted, but You love me,

Unwanted, just a memory.

Though You died, You rose again, washing away all my sin.

And now You'll never let me go.

I'm with You eternally so, I'm not unwanted.

No, I'm not unwanted!

You're not *unwanted*!

Do you believe me?

IN UNWANTED WORDS

If you have made it this far in the book, then you have read a story that may be hard for many of you to believe. As I wrote down my journey, it was hard for me to look at, remember and even fathom that I had been through so much in my life. I regret and am very sorrowful that I had hurt so many people while I was on this quest to find myself. Not all of them that I hurt were mentioned in this book. I pray that everyone has been or will be healed from the wounds that they received from me.

As you can see, I believed that I was living a lie. So, I told everyone the lie that I believed that I was living. I was a gay man who was trying to live a straight life with a woman. My feelings and desires were real. I didn't choose them. I would *never* choose to be gay.

As you read, I believe homosexual acts are a symptom of the disease of sin (flesh) we are all born with, thanks to Adam. When I prayed for God to take the symptom away, He didn't. For example, if I had symptoms that revealed that I had cancer, I would be thankful for them. These manifested symptoms may have saved my life depending on how early I may have found out about my disease.

From a psychological standpoint, I believe that I became homosexual because I detached from my masculinity at an early age. One way that I did it was by rejecting my father. Also, by vowing not to be like men because I thought they were weak. Finally, by wanting to be like my mom. I don't believe I was completely detached because I didn't believe that I was a woman trapped in a man's body. There were a few times that I fantasized about being a woman, but that was very short-lived.

I went to another counselor sometime later in my life. At our first meeting, I gave him a book on defensive detachment that a psychoanalyst had written. I told him that I would like to approach my counseling from this lady's approach. It was very arrogant on my part, but he was very humble in his response to me. He read that book, and that's how he approached my treatment.

On my next visit to his office, he asked me to see if I could recognize any traits or likenesses that I possessed that were like my dad's. His challenge went right through me. Immediately, I became upset. I didn't want to do what he was asking of me.

I rebuked him by saying that I didn't want to do it. He gently reminded me that I had asked him to use the Christian book that I had given him. He held it up in his hand and told me that he was doing exactly what I had asked him to do. Now that I was embarrassed and humbled, I was determined to complete the assignment he gave me. I found out that I had some characteristics of my dad that I had never seen until I was encouraged to look for them in myself. I told you this to help you see how much I had rejected my father. Also, I believe that when we reject God, we reject some parts of us that are like Him because we were made in His image.

If I had fully detached from my masculinity, I might have continued to act like my mom for the rest of my life. But all I would have been doing was *acting* like someone that I wasn't. I could have dressed up in her clothes, worn make-up like her, fixed my hair like her, tried to walk and talk like her, but I was never going to be her. I could have even had surgeries to make me look exactly like her, but underneath it all, I would still be myself on the inside.

I am fully embracing the man that God wanted me to be all along. That is who I want to be for the rest of my life. Now, if I am tempted to lust after a man, I ask God to show me what lie I am still believing. If there isn't a lie, the reason might be that I am momentarily tempted to embrace a familiar pattern of behavior that's been mine for over forty years. Another reason I could be tempted is because I haven't completely reattached to my masculinity yet. I don't fear temptations anymore, though. I am trusting God that I will see the fullness of His salvation in the land of the living.

In Hebrews 10:39 (NASB), the writer wrote this verse I am holding onto by faith until I take my last breath:

"But we are not of those who shrink back to destruction, but of those who have faith to the preserving of the soul."

Another one of my favorite verses is Philippians 1:6 (NASB), where Paul wrote:

"For I am confident of this very thing, that He who began a good work in you will perfect it until the day of Christ Jesus."

IN OTHER WORDS

I want to address some of what is happening in our culture today. The statements I am about to make are not political. These are just my observations. Some of you may get offended. Some of you may agree with me. Some of you may not care in the least about what is going on in our world today.

In the book of Ecclesiastes, Solomon wrote in chapter 1, verse 9 (NASB), "That which has been is that which will be, and that which has been done is that which will be done. So, there is nothing new under the sun."

I want to say that the LGBT community that rioted back in June of 1969 reacted in a totally understandable way to what was happening to them at that time. People were being beaten, bashed, and some even killed back in those days. Just about anyone who is attacked and backed into a corner would react by fighting back in similar circumstances.

Our Declaration of Independence states that we hold these truths to be self-evident, that all men are created equal, that they are endowed with certain unalienable rights, that among these are life, liberty, and the pursuit of happiness.

Definitely, this community has won many battles to ensure that they are being treated like any other human being in America. I am grateful because I benefitted from their efforts when I was in the lifestyle.

Today, I believe equality for everyone has been achieved in most areas of life. But in this case, it's not only been achieved, but I believe things have gone way beyond by leveraging the guise of compassion. Jesus does love *everyone* because the Bible says so. He died for the sins of the whole world, which includes the LGBTQIA+ community. Opening his mouth, Peter said, "I most certainly understand that God is not one to show *partiality*, but in every nation the man who *fears* Him and does what is *right* is welcome to Him" (Acts 10:34–35, NASB).

This community's (I believe it's just a small percentage and not the whole) agenda has pushed American parents and lawmakers into a corner. They are responding out of love and concern for their children. Their demanding that their young children no longer be exposed to the gay rhetoric that is being pushed in public schools or public venues isn't a hateful response in any way. God has entrusted parents to protect their kids.

In the past, children were introduced to the topic of sexuality at an age when it was appropriate for them. Today, they are being introduced to sexuality and transgender curriculums at ages when they aren't mentally or emotionally ready to deal with this kind of information, let alone embrace it.

There are age restriction laws that have been put in place for a reason. You must be a certain age before you are allowed to drink alcohol, smoke, vote, enlist in the army, and have sex with an adult. Why would we ever think that age restrictions shouldn't apply when attempting to prescribe someone hormone blockers before or during puberty? Even more so, what about important prohibitions banning surgical procedures being performed on boys' genitalia and breast implants or with girls' breasts being removed and their genitalia reconstructed?

What I meant by erroring on the side of compassion is that I believe some of the people who are pushing very hard to reach kids at an early age are a result of what they experienced in their childhoods. Many of them do not want anyone to have to endure what they went through. I am in total agreement with not wanting anyone to suffer or to be bullied because of their sexual desires, gender dysphoria, or anything else for that matter! Children need a safe place to be able to discuss their feelings. However, they do not need someone trying to convince them that they are transgender just because they are feeling different. They are still too young to understand the ramifications of transitioning. There are many who are speaking out in anger about having been led to transition when they were in their early teens.

Because of television shows like *Ellen, Will and Grace*, along with movies like *Brokeback Mountain*, many have had their eyes opened. Hearts have been filled with compassion and acceptance. I am thankful that the LGBTQIA+ communities are being valued as human beings. Government officials, celebrities, professional athletes, and even many churches are among those who are very supportive to this community. Times have changed dramatically since I was a teenager and young adult.

Gay and transgender people may be able to convince everyone that they were born that way. All churches may decide to believe this doctrine too. There's still Someone else who must be persuaded. I remember asking God if He was sure that we didn't mutate or maybe something genetically may have caused some people to become gay. He has never confirmed my theory. I don't believe He ever will.

As I told you, I believe God forms us in our mothers' wombs. I believe that takes place right at conception. There are numerous things that can happen during a woman's pregnancy that God never intends to happen. For example, my ex-wife's preeclampsia and toxemia were not the will of God for her, but she got sick. There are things that can cause birth defects along with other developmental issues, such as a child being born intersex (which is very rare). Because of sin (the fall of Adam), we all suffer. Unfortunately, innocent babies in the womb aren't exempt.

The one thing we all have in common is the flesh (sinful nature). I believe it is the responsible party behind all of the confusion in this arena. I believe our flesh receives help from the demonic realm also. For argument's sake, even if we are born that way (I don't believe that is the truth), Jesus said that we must be *born again* (John 3:7).

Some years ago, I read an article that was targeting ex-gay ministries. The journalist said that it looked as if these ministries were making money by selling books along with the other resources that they were promoting. The article said that these ministries were lying to everyone, making false claims that people can change. Some of the authors of these books were lying. I don't believe all of them were, though.

As far as making money, the U.S. Sex Reassignment Surgery Market Report, 2022–2023, states that the market size value in 2022 is USD 2.1 billion. The revenue forecast for 2030 is USD 5.0 billion. I didn't look up what the ex-gay ministry revenues were in the past. Now, many of them have closed their doors, including Exodus. I do not believe that by combining all of their revenue streams, the total amount would be anything close to the staggering numbers of money that is being made in the sex reassignment surgery industry in the United States.

I find it very odd that all of a sudden, large corporations have been willing to risk taking big hits financially to push an agenda that they never had until recently. For instance, the beer company that had a marketing campaign featuring a transgender spokesperson. It received all kinds of backlash. So did the professional baseball team in California when they promoted Pride Month at their stadium. These are just a couple of examples, but there were more than just these two. I find this very strange. I am not claiming to be a conspiracy theorist, but something seems to be off.

"And He found in the temple those who were selling oxen and sheep and doves, and the *money changers* seated at their tables. And He made a scourge of cords, and drove them all out of the temple, with the sheep and the oxen; and He poured out the coins of the *money changers* and overturned their tables; and those who were selling doves He said, 'Take these things away; stop making My Father's house a place of business'" (John 2:14–16, NASB).

If you remember, I told you that God reminded me that preaching, singing, or talking *about* Him isn't the same thing as doing these things *for* Him. Don't be deceived or deceive yourselves.

I want to say that I am aware that there are concerns about people who have gender dysphoria possibly taking their own lives if they don't transition. I am not turning a blind eye to those who are struggling or trying to be insensitive.

However, one recent article that was published stated that the suicide rate was 3.5 times higher for those who have transitioned than the general population. Some of the reasons for this statistic could be due to post-surgical depression. Depression could be brought on because of some surgical complications that can occur. If I considered transitioning, I would certainly research all aspects that have happened or could happen before I moved forward.

Another reason for someone's depression could be that someone has an expectation that becoming someone other than who they were born biologically will make them happy. When that necessarily doesn't happen, then they might lose hope of ever finding happiness.

From my own experience, I wasn't gender dysphoric, but I believed that I was only going to be happy if I was in a gay relationship. I had several, and they didn't make me happy. I don't believe any of us know what will actually make us happy.

"For whoever wishes to save his life will lose it; but whoever loses his life for My sake will find it" (Matthew 16:25, NASB).

The gospel talks about becoming a *new* creation in Christ. God gives many of those who are born-again a *new* name. There are several examples of this happening in the Bible where He did so.

I believe many people might fantasize about becoming someone different than who they are. They may not believe they are someone trapped in the wrong body, but they may not like who they are. I believe that the sinful nature (flesh) that resides in all of us has kept us from being who we *really* are. Once the flesh has been crucified, then we can be the people that God intended for us to be from the beginning.

The One who designed mankind fully understands everything about us. We have emotions and feelings because that's how He made us. Jesus lived in this fallen world. He knows what it's like for us.

"Do not be conformed to this world, but be *trans*formed by the renewing of your mind, so that you may prove what the will of God is, that which is good and acceptable and perfect" (Romans 12:2, NASB).

You might be saying that God is asking us to do the impossible! You would be correct in that statement. What He is asking is impossible to do *without* Him. But *with* Him, all things are possible!

Is anything too difficult for the Lord? (Genesis 18:14, NASB)

IN HIS WORDS

"Now when they heard this, they were pierced to the heart, and said to Peter and the rest of the apostles, 'Brethren, what shall we do?' Peter said to them, 'Repent, and each of you be baptized in the name of Jesus Christ for the forgiveness of your sins; and you will receive the gift of the Holy Spirit'" (Acts 2:37–38, NASB).

Repent (metanoia) means to change in one's way of life resulting from penitence or spiritual conversion. Penitence is the action of feeling or showing sorrow and regret for having done wrong. Your whole mindset changes regarding what you have done. Now, you are in agreement with what God says about the sin you were committing.

"For the sorrow that is according to the *will* of God produces repentance without regret, leading to salvation, but the sorrow of the world produces death" (2 Corinthians 7:10, NASB).

The difference is worldly sorrow is being sorry that you got caught, and Godly sorrow is that you are grieved that you have sinned against God.

I recommend that you pray and ask God to give you understanding in the matter of salvation. There are many opinions and teachings on this subject. Do you believe it would be wise to get your question answered by God or by some theologian who may not have received revelation from the Holy Spirit?

I believe there is a big difference between someone striving to live righteously by the fear of the Lord and by the power of His Spirit, and someone who has said a prayer and then lives according to his sinful desires in a life of willfully sinning.

"For if we go on sinning willfully after receiving the knowledge of the truth, there no longer remains a sacrifice for sins, but a terrifying expectation of judgment and the fury of a *fire* which will consume the adversaries" (Hebrews 10:26, NASB).

"Be on your guard! If your brother sins, rebuke him; if he *repents* forgive him. And, if he commits sins against you seven times a day, and returns to you seven times, saying, "I *repent,*" *forgive* him" (Luke 17: 3–4, NASB).

"If My people, who are called by My name humble themselves and pray and seek My face and turn from their wicked ways, then I will hear from heaven, will forgive their sin and will heal their land" (2 Chronicles 7:14, NASB).

I believe that Scripture describes *repentance* better than most that I have read in the Bible.

One of the popular teachings today is that if you say a prayer, you are saved. These teachers believe that once you are saved, you are always saved. I agree that you have the assurance of salvation as long as you are living a life of repentance by the power of the Holy Spirit. If you are living in the flesh, yielding to its passions and lusts, then you are in danger of eternal destruction unless you repent.

"Everyone, who competes in the games, exercises self-control in all things. They do it to receive a perishable wreath (crown), but we an imperishable. Therefore, I run in such a way, as not beating the air; but I discipline my body and make it my slave, so that, after I have *preached to others*, I myself will not be *disqualified*" (1 Corinthians 9:25–27, NASB).

This is a warning to every believer, but even more to those who are in ministry. We aren't exempt just because we are preaching the gospel. We will be held accountable for whether or not we are living righteously. Teachers are held to a higher standard, not a lower one.

"Let not many of you become teachers, my brethren, knowing that as such we will incur a stricter judgment" (James 3:1, NASB).

We better be sure that what we are teaching is God's word and

His wisdom instead of man's or a devil's teaching.

The Bible says that Jesus will save us from our sins. (Matthew 1:21, NASB).

This scenario should give you *pause* to meditate about some of the doctrines that are being believed today.

Suppose a man is imprisoned for going into a rage and committing murder. He has been sentenced to be executed. A compassionate man petitions the judge by offering to take the convicted murderer's place. He is awarded to be a substitutionary replacement by the court.

The compassionate man takes the punishment of death on himself instead of the murderer who is currently on death row. While in prison, the killer was taught how to manage his anger before he was released. The killer understands how he can control his raging in order to not be violent and repeat what he had done in the past.

However, he ignores his *ability to have self-control* and kills someone again. What do you think will happen to this man?

"But I say, walk by the Spirit, and you will not *carry out* the desire of the flesh" (Galatians 5:16, NASB).

That is a promise that was written down for us by the apostle Paul. By faith, we walk in the Spirit, believing that He gives us the power to overcome *all* of our temptations.

Unless many *repent* of their current lifestyles of sin (not just those bound in homosexuality), then we are headed for destruction as a nation. Not only our nation, because it appears the whole world is following after their own lusts. They are doing whatever seems right in their own eyes.

> For the mystery of lawlessness is already at work; only He who now restrains will do so until He is taken out of the way. Then, that lawless one will be revealed

whom the Lord will slay with the breath of His mouth and bring to an end by the appearance of His coming; that is the one whose coming is in accord with the activity of Satan, with all power and signs and false wonders, and with the deception of wickedness for those who *perish*, because they did not *receive* the love of the *truth* so as to be saved. For this reason, God will send upon them a deluding influence so that they will *believe* what is *false*, in order that they all may be judged who did not *believe* the *truth*, but took *pleasure in wickedness*.

2 Thessalonians 2:7–12, NASB

I believe those days are fast approaching if they are not already at the door. There has been such an acceleration of evil in the past few decades. Again, like in the days of Jonah, Nineveh repented, and God relented. If America doesn't repent, we will be destroyed. If the world doesn't repent, they will be destroyed too.

Then the Lord said, "My Spirit will not always strive with man forever" (Genesis 6:3, NASB).

This Old Testament passage compares with Paul's statement in 2 Thessalonians (NASB), referencing; "*where He who now restrains will do so until He is taken out of the way.*" God is not going to watch us self-destruct (destroy ourselves) forever. One day, the Father is going to look to His right hand. He is going to say that it's time to return to earth. Just as in Noah's day, every intent of the thoughts of man's heart was only evil continually (Genesis 6:5). And the Lord said, "The outcry of Sodom and Gomorrah is indeed great, and their sin is exceedingly grave. I will go down now and see if they have done entirely according to its outcry, which has come to Me; and if not, I will know" (Genesis 18:20–21, NASB).

God is trying to move all of us off of a road that is leading to destruction, and put us on a path of righteousness that is leading to everlasting life.

Jesus said, "Enter through the narrow gate; for the gate is broad that leads to *destruction*, and there are *many* who enter through it. For the gate is small and the way is narrow that leads to life, and there are *few* who find it" (Matthew 7:13–14, NASB).

Now, I want to tell you more about how the Holy Spirit's revelation has increased my belief. He has given me the hope that I stand on and the faith that I live by every day.

"Fixing our eyes on Jesus, the author and perfecter of faith, who for the joy set before Him endured the cross, despising the shame, and has sat down at the right hand of the throne of God. For consider Him who has endured such hostility by sinners against Himself, so that you will not grow weary and lose heart" (Hebrews 12:2–3, NASB).

Jesus was the Son of man who was made in the likeness of sinful flesh. This understanding has given me so much hope and faith. He did everything by the power of the Holy Spirit and not by His own power. That revelation is something to shout about if you comprehend it.

Have you read the scene where Jesus is walking on the water? "Peter says, Lord, if it is You, command me to come to You on the water." And He said, "Come!" (Matthew 14:28, NASB). Peter walked out onto the water in obedience and faith. He received the word *Come* from the Word of God (Jesus).

He saw the *Son of Man* doing the impossible. As long as he believed that he could do what Jesus was doing, then he stayed on top of the water. As soon as he became frightened, he began to sink. Jesus saved him from drowning. Then, Jesus said to him, "You of little faith, why did you *doubt*?"

We can accomplish everything the Father has put us here on earth to accomplish, just like Jesus did. He had every opposition imaginable, but He still fulfilled the Father's will. We can do the *same* thing.

Jesus said, "Truly, truly, I say to you, he who *believes* in Me, the works that I do, he will do also; and greater works than these he will do; because I go to the Father. Whatever you ask in My name, that will I do, so that the Father may be glorified in the Son. If you ask Me anything in My name, I will do it" (John 14:12–14, NASB).

That is some promise that He made! I believe Him. Do you believe Him?

"And Jesus said to him, 'If you can? All things *are possible* to him who *believes.*'" (Mark 9:23, NASB).

I have finished what God has asked me to do. I have shared my story with you, along with the revelations that the Holy Spirit has given me. You don't have to *take* my word for it, but you do have to *take* Him at His word!

"For thou hast magnified thy *word* above all thy *name*" (Psalm 138:2, KJV).

"Heaven and earth will pass away, but My words will not pass away" (Matthew 24–35, NASB).

"Behold, I am coming quickly, and My reward is with Me, to render every man according to what he had done" (Revelation 22:12, NASB).

In these last days, He is crying out to all the *unwanted* outcasts to come into His kingdom.

"Therefore, be on the alert, for you do not know which day your Lord is coming" (Matthew 24:42, NASB).

Jesus is coming soon…Will you be ready?